THE UNLIKELY
Olympian

STEP INTO YOUR FEARS TO
ACHIEVE YOUR DREAM

DANIELLE KETTLEWELL

THE UNLIKELY OLYMPIAN

Step into Your Fears to Achieve Your Dream

Published by Celebrity Publishers
USA +1 702 997 2229
Australia +61 2 8005 4878
enquiries@celebritypublishers.com

To Bulk order books inquire at:
www.daniellekettlewell.com/contact

To Hire Danielle Kettlewell For Speaking:
www.daniellekettlewell.com/speaking

DEDICATION

To the child inside all of us that believes in a dream.

TABLE OF CONTENTS

ACKNOWLEDGEMENTS

To the two people who made everything in my life possible by willing me into existence – Mum and Dad - thank you for giving me the gift of life in this lifetime. You are my biggest role models and have shown me how to become the hardworking, loving, open minded and tenacious woman that I am today. Thank you for creating our beautiful family and raising us all in the values to love, gratitude, kindness and faith. I couldn't be prouder to have you as my parents. I love you endlessly.

To my second set of 'parents', my siblings – Damian, Monique, Matthew and Genevieve. You have loved me and raised me as your own. You have always looked out for me and wanted the best for me. You have been guiding lights in my life, always helping direct me on the right path. The age-gap between us gave me the perspective to see the world in a different light to help expand my mind. Thank you for bringing each and every one of my nieces and nephews into the world and making me the proudest Aunt. I love you all always.

To my bonus siblings, my in-laws – Charlene, Mike, Jennifer and Geoff. Thank you for loving my brothers and sisters. You have all watched me grow up, and to me you have always been blood. I love you all eternally.

To my fourteen, once little, now not so little, humans who were my inspiration; Meleah, Charlotte, Thomas, Rebecca, Ivy, Rosie, Parker, Noel, Sawyer, Rowan, Scarlette, Ruby, Ollie and Noah. Moving across the world, away from all of you when you were growing up, was heart-wrenching, but I wanted to show you by example that you can do whatever you are passionate about in this lifetime. And maybe a little bit of me wanted to be your cool Aussie Aunty DanDan. Remember that even though I am far away – I love you all forever.

To my gals who have a piece of my heart – Mara, Stephanie, Natalie, Jess, Erica, Kelli and Elise . I couldn't have been blessed with better best friends growing up. We have laughed together, cried together and travelled together. We have been there for the ups and downs, for the stupid moments and the profound ones, for all the craziness of life. Thank you for believing in me before I believed in myself and always keeping me grounded. I love you all infinitely.

To everyone in the synchro community – every coach who ever coached me, every teammate I ever swam with, every judge who ever judged me, every volunteer who ever helped me out, every board member who helped look out for the best interest in me. To the Arbutus Club synchro girls, to VPW, to PEM, to WCS, SN, Synchro WA and Synchro Australia. To my duet partner, Ethan, who took a leap of faith with me to make history in our little sport. Thank you to you all. Thank you all for inspiring my love in synchro and in people. The community that we are all engulfed in is so passionate, creative and fueled by love. Thank you to all of the people in Canada, Denmark and Australia who have accepted me as one of your own. We are so lucky to be a part of the greatest sport in this world. I can't wait for synchro to receive more of the shine that it deserves.

To my sport psychs, Brian & Matt. Thank you for giving me the tools to be able to perform at a level I never knew was possible. Your experience, advice and understanding helped me create the mind of an elite athlete.

To my synchro soul sisters, my Aussie National teammates and especially my Olympic teammates– Amie, Rose, Bianca, Deb, Nikita, Cristina, Hannah & Emily. I feel so blessed to have been able to go on that journey with you all. It was such a wonderous journey, but what made it magic was experiencing it with you. To Roslyn, Mary and especially Lilianne – thank you helping and pushing us to be the best versions of ourselves – thank you, I love you all continuously.

To Lexi. I know it wasn't always easy, but you stood by me with unwavering support the entire time. I know you didn't do it for the acknowledgement, and I know you don't like thanks, but know I am forever grateful for you.

To my Perth soul-family, who have come into my life after a difficult time and through shining in their own true power have invigorated me to be the best version of myself. I am so boundlessly grateful for each and every interaction with you that has inspired my faith in humans in this universe. Thank you for existing in my life and believing in me. I send my love to you all.

To my firecracker of a housemate – Becky-boo. Thank you for loving me through this entire journey since we met, especially my writing journey. The universe brought us together to support each other on the path to our dreams. You have taught me how to live in my truth and how to love myself through your example. I appreciate every moment of lost sleep from late night soul chats and belly laughs. I can't wait to see where life takes us. I love you unwaveringly.

To the kindred spirit that shot out of the stars and into my life – Luka. You see straight into my soul with more truth than anyone ever has. You challenge me, inspire me and lift me up to let me shine on my own two feet. Thank you for coming into my life so that we can see the world through a whole new set of glasses. I don't know where this universe will take us but I can't wait to do it all by your side − I am eternally grateful for every passing moment together. My love for you surpasses the barricades of this lifetime.

And lastly but definitely not least − to every person out there who believes there is something greater in this life for them. I was a nobody in an extremely difficult sport who did something greater than my wildest dreams could ever imagine. I did it, so I KNOW you can do it too. I have written this book for you. You are special. You are enough and you are meant to make something of yourself. This world wants to see you thrive. I want to see you thrive. But before any of that ever happens − you need to believe in the power inside. When that happens, the magic starts to unfold.

ABOUT THE AUTHOR

Danielle Kettlewell was born and raised in Vancouver, Canada, as the youngest of five children, to Australian parents. At the age of eight years old she started the sport of artistic swimming, commonly known as synchro. Eventually she fell in love with the little-known sport, however, she had one big problem – she just wasn't that talented at synchro. With that belief, Danielle 'retired'

at the age of 18 to pursue her undergraduate education. A few years later, her life was turned upside down when she received a bad concussion, causing her to drop out of university and put her life on hold. But then an unbelievable opportunity came her way to move to Australia to try out for the Australian national team in hopes of qualifying for the Olympic games. Despite the improbable circumstances and doubt surrounding her, Danielle set out for Australia to go after an impossible dream. Through incredible courage, relentless optimism and an unwavering desire to overcome adversity, Danielle made her impossible dream a reality in 2016 when she competed at the Rio Olympics. Through her unlikely journey to the Olympic Games Danielle became determined to share her journey with others, not for her own benefit, but to inspire others to go after their dreams, however unlikely they might seem.

After five years on the Australian National synchro team Danielle ended her sporting career by making history competing as Australia's First Mixed Duet at the 2019 FINA World Championships. Recently, she left the world of synchro to go after her next dream of helping others achieve their own dreams. Danielle now spends her time sharing her message through speaking at schools, work places and conferences, and coaching others to break through the invisible boundaries of fear that hold them back.

If you are wanting to work with Danielle personally to understand how to go after your own dreams find more information at:

www.daniellekettlewell.com

NOTE

This book has been written from the perspective of my personal experience. I am proud of every word that I have written and will stand by with unwavering faith that my intention is to share my journey through my opinion, so that the message can resonate with others to go after their dreams. Nevertheless, every story has two sides and although I tried to write as objectively as possible, I have changed some individuals names to protect everyone involved. I ask you to read with an open heart, mind and soul, understanding that everyone is on their own journey, and this is just a story about a part of mine.

August 5th, 2016

The buses lined up by the hundreds, waiting for athletes by the dozens to pile in for the drive to the main arena. Everywhere you looked, people were lined up in matching uniforms, patriotically displaying the names of their countries. The energy felt electric. I eagerly wished the time would pass quicker so we could walk into the stadium sooner, while also wanting to capture every moving second.

As the never-ending queue of buses flew down the highway, the opposing traffic waited at a standstill for the elite guests to pass. I felt like we were royalty. In this moment, in this place, at this time – we were.

Upon arrival, we all piled out of the buses and lined up by country, wrapping ourselves around the stadium. Because Australia was at the beginning of the alphabet, we were right near the front. The first big country to walk in, a badge of honour that we all wore with pride.

Thinking of all my friends and family around the world, eagerly waiting to see a glimpse of my face on TV, made my palms sweat with excitement. I was doing everything I could to not bounce with elation.

As our Aussie conglomerate glided closer to the main entrance, the ecstatic roar of the crowd inside started to vibrate through us. The line was leading us down through a dark tunnel with a burst of light teasing its way through the blackness in the distance. I grabbed my teammate's hand as we obediently followed our flag-bearer into the darkness. The buzz of the crowd cheering inside initiated a euphoric and harmonized patriotic cheer from my country's fellow athletes. "Aussie, Aussie, Aussie," bellowed one booming voice. "Oi Oi Oi" we all responded. Over and over again we cheered, singing out the call of our country from the very depths of our souls.

Hot tears poured down my face. Flashbacks of all my moments of doubt, all my sacrifices, all the times when I picked myself off the floor, defeated, and encouraged myself to get back up. Every moment I consciously chose inspiration, motivation and optimism over the impossible opposite. Everything I had done for years upon years to bring myself here, played through my head. I was never meant to be here, but yet here I was – walking into the **Opening Ceremony at the Olympic Games**.

INTRODUCTION

I was never going to be an Olympian.

Hold up. I know what you are thinking. *"But you are?"*

Let me explain.

I was always the bigger girl, the awkward girl. The one who was a great team player but, let's be honest, everyone knew I wasn't going anywhere. I was the one who wasn't really that good at my sport, but I did it because I loved it. And for me, that was enough. It made me happy, brought me joy and purpose. It filled me up and, most of all, I was so darn passionate about it. But I was never going to make anything of myself in the sport. I knew that.

Or so I thought.

So in 2013, when I got the outrageous opportunity, as a concussed, unfit, university dropout in Vancouver, Canada to go to Australia and try out for the Aussie National Synchronized Swimming team the day after my 21st birthday - I thought that I was existing in some parallel Universe!

Me. Little ol', me – the synchro swimmer who "retired" at 18 and never thought she was good enough, going after this! It was crazy! Impossible! Who was I to do that?

The day I stood there over skype and heard those words, I immediately counted myself out. Who was I to go and do something that crazy? I would never be good enough. Why even try? And just imagine what everyone was going to think of me if I did? They would all judge me. I knew it.

As I let the thought marinate in my concussed mind and battled all the limiting self-beliefs that were holding me back, I heard a little whisper inside my soul. A little whisper that said to me – *What if?*

What if I tried? What if I just went and gave it a hot shot? And what if… no, no, NO WAY…but maybe… what if I was just good enough? What if I made it to the Olympics?

That "what if" stuck with me. It planted itself inside my brain and attached itself to my heart. I looked forward and imagined watching the 2016 Rio Olympic Games on TV. I imagined how I would feel in the two different circumstances – if I tried, or if I didn't. And I realized that…

> **I would rather**
> **try and "fail" than always wonder**
> **– "what if"?**

That thought, that belief, that little inkling of a whisper inside me set me off on a journey to achieve, what I call, *an impossible dream.*

As I inched closer and closer to making that dream a reality, I realized that I was making it happen! Little ol' me. But more importantly than that, I realized that this was waaayy bigger than me.

I believe that the universe, God, creator, source, mother earth – whoever you choose to believe in – gave me the chance to pursue my insane Olympic opportunity not for me, but to share my story and, more importantly, share what I learned, so that YOU can achieve your dreams too.

Sure, it feels good to have gone to the Olympics and become the person that I am today through that experience. But you know what feels great? Contribution.

Knowing that it's not about, and never was about, just me; but rather about how I can add value to this planet we are living on. How I can make this earth just a little bit better for others when I leave this physical realm.

That is my next passionate dream I am working to accomplish through the clarity that I found by going to the Olympics.

We are living in a time when we have the world at our fingertips. All the simple tasks that humans used to spend their days doing to stay alive hundreds of years ago have been atomized, broken down and made easy so that WE can live out our purpose.

If you are reading this book I bet you are one of the lucky ones in this world who doesn't have to hunt, gather and find your own food. You don't need to walk countless miles every day to search for water to nourish your family. Sometimes it's so easy for us to get wrapped up in our daily lives and forget how lucky we all are! How lucky we are to be able to wake up and not worry about the basic necessities that keep us alive as human beings. How lucky we are to be able to breathe, see, feel, hear and love in this lifetime of ours!

The generations before us have paved the way SO that we all have the freedom and opportunity to go after what sets our soul on fire and make our difference in our little part of the world.

Not everyone is going to be Oprah, become the prime minister or start a not-for-profit. Maybe you are. Maybe you are not. But

YOUR job, your obligation in this world if you are reading this, is to open your eyes, trust your heart and step into the power that is inside you to **go after your dreams!**

Maybe your dream is to be the best mother or father you can be in this world, maybe it is to be the best employee, scientist, or engineer. Or maybe it is to start your own business, be a speaker, actress, singer or even write a book. But if it makes you happy, truly happy; the type of happiness where you wake up with light in your eyes and a stride in your step - know that that is enough. That is your job. That is your obligation.

Don't compare yourself to anyone else. Don't even think about it. You will be tempted. We all are. I definitely am, all the time! But remember that...

> ## Comparison is the thief of joy
> ### and
> ### the only person you should ever compare yourself to is the person you believe you can be.

Who is the person that I believe I can be? It is someone that sets out on her next dream of inspiring others to go after theirs. A person that shares her love and light with the world, because I know it is inside me and just waiting for the chance to shine on others. And even if that means I only help one person find their glow – that is enough for me. Because that makes me happy, that makes me fulfilled.

There I said it. That was scary. It always is. But let me tell you – when you put it out there, say it out loud to the world and let the universe know what you want to do with it AND follow your CLARITY – the universe will conspire to make it happen.

Don't trust me that it's possible yet? Don't worry we will get there together. Because I have exciting news for you. Yup. For you.

You have just found your new best friend, confidant, motivator and biggest cheerleader. Me!

Hi. Welcome. My name is Danielle Kettlewell. Call me DK ;)

I am here for you.

But more importantly, I am here to show you that you can make it happen.

I am going to show, through the story of my journey, how you can find C.L.A.R.I.T.Y and achieve your most unlikely dreams.

Grab your Manifesting your Dreams Visualization at www.DKbonuses.com

Chapter 1

C – CLEAR ON YOUR LIMITING SELF-BELIEFS

Now before we set out on an epic journey towards our dreams together I want to make sure that we have a few things are really clear. This is going to take work. Don't expect to just read this book and hope that you will magically fall into your ideal life in all aspects. To find the C.L.A.R.I.T.Y. in your life you will need to challenge yourself and implement it.

You see my friends, every cell in my body wants this to be your reality so I want to set you up for the greatest level of success. To get to that success, though, you need to understand that there are conditions. Aspects along the journey that we need to realize are not a detour but rather PART of the process. Let's call these guys our – **speed bumps**. Before you put expectations on yourself that you are going to finish this book and accomplish it all easy-peasy-lemon-squeezy, know that

> 1. It will not be linear.
> 2. It will have setbacks.
> 3. It doesn't always fit YOUR time limit.

These little guys may be intimidating but they are not scary, I promise – they are BEAUTIFUL! If you ever hit a bump in your road, you can take in a big sigh of relief and know that it is all good! You haven't "failed" but rather you are just being challenged in the process. And at the end of the day those challenges are just going to make you stronger in the end, because that is what challenge and adversity does. It's the worlds way of testing the fire in your heart to go after your dream. You see because many will be too overwhelmed by the bumps in the road. They will take them as a bad sign, then back down and walk away. But they couldn't be more wrong. It's this world's way of sifting through those who have set forth on the path with a blazing heart of passion from the ones who can be easily swayed and aren't standing in their truest passion.

That is why it is not supposed to be.

▶ LINEAR

You may think that your dream will have this one directional path to "success". For some of you, maybe it will. But for most of you – it won't. There will be twists and turns along the way. There will be times when you feel like you are on the right route, perfectly following the GPS instructions, and there will be other times where you will be lost and wondering how the heck you ended up doing three loops and coming back to the same spot?

It is okay. It is normal to get lost. In those times of turmoil, sit back and remind yourself of the power of your dream. Know that everyone who has ever done anything extraordinary has never followed a direct line to success. There will be twists, turns and points where you are going to feel like you have been flipped upside down. But stay the course, embrace the speedbumps and remember that they are part of the path to the dream and not a detour from it.

▸ SETBACKS

I like to call them setbacks. Many people like to call them failures. It's all about your perception of those setbacks and how you are going to use them to push forward.

The only true "failure" is when you choose to LET IT defeat you. With these setbacks, take them as a learning opportunity and know that not only are they NORMAL − but they are NEEDED for the process. Because those setbacks give us the opportunity to sit down and have a look at what we can do better for next time when we get back up.

It's this world's way of testing you to see if you REALLY want it. If you are willing to push yourself past the small blockages along the way, remind yourself of the dream and put yourself back in the game.

▸ TIME LIMITS

Have you heard of SMART goals? Specific. Measurable. Achievable. Result-oriented. Time-limited. Yah, well this little guy refers to the T.

Now don't get me wrong − setting a time-limit on a goal or a dream is helpful. I couldn't have just gotten to the Rio Olympics whenever I wanted. I needed to be good enough to get there by 2016. But often these little goals of ours like room to expand and move when they feel like it. They don't always like to be bound down by a specific time they need to be achieved by - to the minute.

Yes. Definitely. Set a date you want to get there by. It's great to work towards − but know that it is OKAY if that date moves.

Maybe it moves forward, maybe back. And if that date moves, remember that is only a **setback** to teach you a lesson you can learn, never a "failure."

When you struggle to understand why that didn't work within your time limit, remind yourself that is it okay, tap into the fire inside of you that fuels your passion, pick yourself back up and keep driving directly into the golden sunset that's glowing its beautiful warm sunlight on your dream.

OKAY! Now that we have the speed bumps identified – let's get to the good stuff. The method. The story. The CLARITY.

> ### C – Clear on your Limiting Self-Belief (LSB)

"We are who we believe we are –
so make sure the belief is in alignment with
your soul's desire to be who
you KNOW you CAN be."

– Danielle Kettlewell

▶ LIMITING SELF-BELIEFS

What is your greatest Limiting Self-Belief (LSB)?

Now that is a massive question to start off with, isn't it?

First of all, you are probably thinking – what is a limiting self-belief? Fair. Completely Fair. I have catapulted you straight into an ocean of interrogation, when you thought you were coming here to read about the journey of how a girl got to the Olympics. We will get there – I promise. Just stay with me.

Our Limiting Self-Beliefs (LSBs) are at the basis of everything that the foundation of our selves live on. They are the pillars that hold us back and drive us forward in humanity. They are why we react to certain situations and retract from others. And the craziest part of it all is that most of us have the same core, foundational limiting self-beliefs:

> I am not enough.
> I am not capable.
> I am not worthy.

Yes, these LSBs may disguise themselves as something else, deep inside us.

- *I am not beautiful.*
- *I am not talented.*
- *I won't be able to do it.*
- *I will be judged.*
- *I don't deserve that man/woman in my life.*
- *I don't have the confidence.*
- *I am being selfish, putting myself before others.*
- *I am too old/fat/ugly/stupid to make it happen.*

Resonate with any of those statements? Yah, I thought so. We all do. And the craziest part of all is that we all walk around this planet thinking that everybody ELSE has it conquered, figured out, is confident, knows what they are doing and doesn't struggle with any of those things that WE struggle with. Because they are OUR thing. Not anyone else's.

Now let me tell you one thing. That is not true. Those are the basis of everyone.

Once we become clear on what are our main LSB, we can understand ourselves on a deeper level and tap into the reasoning behind how, and why we do everything in our life.

My LSB? That I am not enough, never was, and never will be enough. Still to this very day, as I sit here and write a book about all of this, I have the niggle of not being enough of a human, soul, author or Olympian to be able to write this book.

If we are lucky, in some situations maybe our LSB doesn't pop in. And for just a split second beyond all of the doubt that exists in us, a little whisper of belief peeps through. The veil drops and we allow ourselves think that maybe, just maybe, we are worthy, we are enough, we are capable?

Then our good old mate – **Who am I?** pops in for a little visit.

▶ WHO AM I?

Who am I to be beautiful? Who am I to be loved? Who I am to deserve that opportunity, take that job, be with that person? Who am I to think that I am crazy enough to dream that big and make that happen?

Well, let me tell you, my friends.

First of all, **Mr. Who am I?** is like that annoying neighbor who keeps popping by when he's are not wanted, but we are too polite to tell him to buzz off. So we just graciously have a little chat with him, then kindly lead him to the door when we have decided we've had enough. But, no matter what, he will keep popping by, usually at the most inconvenient of times. We just need to remember to NOT invite him in for a tea - which turns into dinner and eventually just ends up with him moving right on in! Because he might as well, when he's coming around so often right? No!

We allow **Who I am?** to come in. It is important in our lives to remember and reflect on why he is visiting and what LSB he is poking at. Then, when we've had our moment of self-awareness, we need to politely lead him to the door and remind ourselves that this house, this brain, this body of ours - belongs to us. And we have the ability to let those thoughts come and go as we please.

Secondly, now that we have dealt with Mr. **Who Am I?** I want to remind you, as your new best friend that you

> **You ARE enough.**
> **You ARE worthy.**
> **You ARE capable.**

I know that you know that. I know that it is deep inside you, maybe way deep inside. But behind all those LSBs. Behind the massive darkness that holds you back from realizing your greatness. When we pull back all of those layers, you know that you are ENOUGH, WORTHY & CAPABLE too.

Maybe it is only 1% of you that knows that, or 0.01%. Or, maybe even 0.0000001%, but deep down there in the depths of your soul – you know. You are enough. You are worthy. You are capable.

We develop all these LSBs through our stories, the ones that make us who we are and the journeys that take us to who we are meant to be. Our childhood, our adulthood, our life. There is no one to blame for causing those LSBs. But they are experiences that lead to the stories, that make up our character. And in those stories, through our character and actions, we feed or starve those LSBs along the way.

Mine? Like I said, "I am not enough."

Now let me tell you the story of, how I got there.

DK with her parents and siblings;
Matthew, Monique, Genevieve & Damian

Number 52. That's me.

November 17th, 1992 I was born as the 52nd grandchild to my maternal grandmother MumMum who loved to play bridge. I was called the Ace of Hearts to top off the lot and gave my grandma a full deck of grandkids. My mum was one of eleven, so it was only natural for her to want a big family as well. Being the youngest of five children always seemed normal to me but I knew that our family was more of an anomaly in our day and age, especially with the age-gap between my siblings and me.

At 21 years old my parents, with my newborn eldest brother in tow, immigrated to Canada from Sydney, Australia, following my Mum's large family who chose Vancouver as a city of opportunity to create a new life for everyone. My Dad was a plumber while my Mum stayed at home taking care of their ever-expanding family. By the time they were 28 they had four kids at home while my Dad was taking night classes to finish his post-secondary schooling and work towards a University diploma. All the while he was also starting a new pub and liquor business. They wanted more kids but didn't have enough time or money to add another one to the mix.

So when that non-drinking, yet street smart, Dad of mine had his business running smoothly and my Mum had successfully transitioned my siblings all into high school, the thought of just one more child was brought into the picture. Even though my Mum was 43 at the time, she willed me into existence from her deep desire to love and bring up another child in this world.

When I was born, my teenage siblings, Gen, Matt, Monique and Damian were all standing there in the room, eagerly awaiting my arrival. Sure the 14 – 21-year age-gap between me and them seemed a little bit odd to some people. Quite often people got confused and thought my Mum was my grandma and my elder brothers and sisters had to constantly reassure their new partners that I wasn't just their secret love child that their parents were raising. But despite all of that – growing up as an "only child", as the youngest of five children was just my normal.

I was a happy-go-lucky kid with not a worry in the world. I was the twinkle in the eyes of my parents and the fun little sister to all my brothers and sisters. As a four-year-old I was living my best life – that was until my niece came along.

Yes, I became an aunty at four years old. A title that I now wear as a badge of honor but getting a four-year-old to understand how they are going to become an aunty when all they associate aunties with is old ladies, is a hard task. I was devastated to say the least. No matter how much I begged or pleaded my Mum and my sister Monique, I just couldn't, for the life of me, understand why I had to be my niece Meleah's aunty and not her big sister.

When Meleah was born she was adorable, with her half Asian mix and big brown eyes. Everyone knew she was beautiful – and when you are a little four year old who used to be the cutest of them all, and realize that your spot on the adorable scale has just been bumped by someone who you don't even get to call your sister – well that's a reality check let me tell you.

Boom. There we go. First recognition of my Limiting Self-Belief (LSB). I am not enough. I am not enough to be her big sister, I am not enough to be the cutest anymore, I am not enough to be the center of attention anymore.

Of course, none of this was true and no one really thought this. It was just my little-headed four-year-old's interpretation of the situation. Am I blaming Meleah or anyone else for having those LSBs develop? Not in the least. It is just life. Was that the exact situation that triggered that LSB? Maybe not. Our LSBs are built up through years of menial situations where our ego takes things a little too personally.

But we all do this in situations, because at the base of everything we are all just four-year-olds who want to be loved, heard and be the center of attention.

Until we develop our self-awareness, as humans we translate situations through an ego-centric mind frame. We think that how people react and interact in situations is how they feel about us when in complete truth it is always just a reflection of how they feel about themselves. That is why, when we are living in the subconscious awareness, we think that every situation has to do with us, we take it a little too personally and boom – there's another tick on the LSB chart.

As a four-year-old, of course, I would not have consciously been questioning whether "I am enough" or not. But that combination of circumstances planted a seed that grew through the experiences of life. As a child, those experiences are unconscious to us, just little seeds buried in the soil that makes us who we are.

That's why, whenever we see little kids, they always walk around oozing confidence. Doing all the things that life hasn't taught them are socially unacceptable yet, like lifting your dress up to show your undies in public, putting your hand down your pants with no worry in the world and going up to strangers and staring at them just a bit too long.

Those seedlings are placed in the subconscious or unconscious part of ourselves and, with time, nourishment and bit of sunlight and experience they prosper – they grow.

What did I do with the seedlings in my subconscious? I fed them.

Literally.

Food. I loved it; I still do. Food was my vice, to comfort my limiting self-beliefs.

▶ VICES

Ahh, the good old fake comfort of a vice, hey? Think of a vice as like a security blanket. A veil of disguise. Fool's gold. They are the things we all like to pretend we don't have a problem with, that we are just letting ourselves enjoy. Because, what is life if we can't enjoy it right?

Ha. But we know we are lying to ourselves. What starts as enjoyment turns into a forced sense of security, a reliance, an unconscious habit that we approach with guilt. And GUILT, oh baby let me tell you, guilt is never a positive feeling to have.

For some of us that vice is alcohol, for others it is gambling, drugs, self-hatred. Addiction is at its darkest core and, luckily, not all of us get there. But, no matter whether it is an addiction or not, it is a coping mechanism for us to deal with ourselves and not address the root of the problem, the most painful part of the issue – the limiting self-belief.

My-oh-my, my vice loooovvvveedd food. That vice of mine was fed, constantly, to fill the void. Chocolate in the morning when I got up, convincing myself I would only have one, then to consume multiple more with so much guilt. Peanut butter, milk and sugar milkshakes in the evening when I was home alone, and I felt like that LSB was consuming me alive with self-hatred. And one, two, three milkshakes were never enough. You get the idea.

What hurts me, now is not the food I consumed, because I know at the end of my life, looking back, I'm not going to regret eating that extra piece of chocolate – but HOW it was consumed. With so much self-hatred, disgust and guilt. Feelings that literally manifest in our body when we hold onto them too long. Emotions that stick with us in the darkest hours of the night, when we wake up in tears from so much self-loathing. I consumed food like that for so many years, with so many low vibrations, sad, heart-aching feelings that make me want to cry when I sit here now and think about them all. The self-hatred and disgust got so bad at points in my teenage years, where I sat there at the kitchen table in the evening when no one was home and held the knife to my wrists, wondering, playing with the thought of "What if I just ended it all now?", because inside my soul it hurt so much. I believed I was so disgusting that there was no point in even being alive, because who in their right mind could ever love me in this state?

▸ LSBS DON'T DISCRIMINATE

I call myself fortunate. I grew up with two loving parents in a safe country, surrounded by siblings who loved me. I never had to worry deeply about my personal safety or stress about how I was going to get my next meal. I am eternally grateful for all of those aspects of my childhood.

But I still have limiting self-beliefs.

These bloody LSBs don't discriminate. They don't care if you had a difficult upbringing or experienced a traumatic event. They exist in all of us. And all of our LSBs can be recognized, acknowledged and overcome – no matter your race, religion, sex, gender or socioeconomic status. But, these LSBs, when not dealt with, grow into weeds that attack all the aspects of our life, when we don't tend to them. And when they attack all aspects of our life – they cause struggle and pain.

We all have struggle and pain inside us, and no one's pain is more or less worthy than anyone else's. The LSBs all start out weighing equally inside all of us. But, on the opposite side of that weight, we feel the potential within us, the potential which can only start to be accessed when we work through our LSBs. And, when we work through our LSBs, then, and only then, the weight of them within us starts to decrease. The only way to lighten that load and lessen that burden in each of us is to acknowledge what it is, where it is coming from and make a choice to not let it dominate our life.

The LSB of the person who is struggling from a difficult upbringing weighs no more than the LSB of a person who is bullied at work. The scales only start to tip to lighten the load when one of the two chooses to work on their LSB and not let it hold them back from their life's dreams and desires.

Like I said, there is no point spending time doing the blame game and pointing fingers at anyone or any situation that caused these LSBs because, if it wasn't from that one circumstance, it would be from another. It was always going to be there – our challenge in life is to learn how to overcome it.

It will keep arising throughout our life, in every situation it possibly can, as a test for us to overcome it again and again. For an opportunity to leap ahead as opposed to being pulled behind.

So, like I said, I fed my limiting self-belief. With food, unkind thoughts and self-hatred. As I grew up, and the circumstances of life consumed those weedy seedlings of LSBs and as my consciousness grew with my age – I grew into the exciting years of teenage-dom – where awakening consciousness meets our limiting self-beliefs at the door, and emotions go wild.

> Those thoughts ate me up for years as I would stand in front of the mirror squeezing my fat with tears rolling down my face wishing for my dear life that I could just cut it all away. Wishing that I was someone else, had someone else's body, wishing that I could just be a different body type so that someone could love me. Because I desperately wanted to be loved, but I never could be, until I loved myself.

> With the beauty of hindsight this adversity was a sign for learning, I just couldn't see it at the moment, as I was trapped in the murky, dark box of my own limiting self-beliefs not allowing myself to see the light. But it was a sign for me to learn my limiting self-beliefs, identify my vices and make

changes so that I could allow my light to shine as brightly as it possibly could when I let it.

In the year after high school, it got to a point where after seeing a photo of myself at my nephew's baptism I was so disgustingly shocked at what I had allowed myself to get to. I spent the entire evening sobbing in self-repulsion. So, I decided to make a change. I decided to learn. I worked extra to afford to hire a personal trainer, behind everyone's back, so that I could transform. I start to fuel myself with love not hate. Kindness not regrets. And it slowly started to work. I started to change on the outside, which helped on the inside but of course it didn't solve the issue. Because the issue was my limiting self-belief.

Within me those limiting self-beliefs chose to surface in the form of:

❯ I am not beautiful.

❯ I am not deserving of love.

❯ I am not the right shape, size, height or weight.

❯ I am not enough.

❯ I am not worthy.

Common LSBs that exist in so many of us, especially women in this media-saturated world. I chose the mirror as a target for my limiting self-beliefs. I decided that my worth was dependent on the physical reflection that mirrored itself back at me. And, like they do, when the weeds of LSBs fester within us – it ate away at me and caused struggle and pain.

That pain led to self-hate and that self-hate led to me decide to use my vice, food, to comfort my LSB. So it just circulated. See, because we will always try to make LSB disappear, we will cover it up and use our vice to make it feel better.

That cycle – LSB trigger – comfort with vice - will continue and continue until we choose to have the awareness to address:

> ### #1 - Our Limiting Self-Belief.
> ### #2 - Our Vice.

Now you are probably thinking, "Well thank you, DK for bringing up all the fun stuff within me." Again, as your new best friend –

you are welcome. But stemming from the impatience that exists in all of us, you are probably wondering – "Great, but how do I move through all this stuff now?"

We are getting there, I promise, but before we can ever move through something we need to be aware of WHAT we are moving through, so – I ask you these questions.

▶ QUESTIONS

⊙ **What is your Limiting Self-Belief?**

⊙ **Can you think of a circumstance in your life that may have been disguised as something else, but really came back to your LSB?**

⊙ **What is/was your vice? (it can be more than one)**

Got it? It's not easy, I know, but you can do it. I believe in you.

Like I said before, behind all those layers of limiting self-beliefs inside all of us there is a whisper. A little tiny whisper of belief. A quiet little voice that, above all else, believes that maybe – just maybe, those LSBs aren't true. Let me tell you something.

> ### Listen to the whisper of truth.

That whisper is the powerful, pure little part of our soul that is tapped into our true potential. Into our complete certainty. Into the knowing that we can be enough, we can be worthy, we can be capable.

But, just like the weed of LSB needs to be fed to grow, so does the seedling of **belief**.

That seedling of belief is the most stunningly beautiful and radiantly gorgeous flower. It is the flower that can blossom so massively and exquisitely that anyone walking by will stop to have a little smell. But flowers can't grow unless they are nourished.

Okay, okay, I hear yah. − "Enough with the plant metaphors, DK! We are not becoming botanists - we are trying to achieve our dreams!" You are right.

▶ BELIEF

At the basis of our limiting self-beliefs is BELIEF. A belief is something that we have developed, based on what we chose to believe about ourselves. So, all we have to do is change that belief. Change that belief and step into our "I Am"s.

> I am enough.
> I am worthy.
> I am capable.

Say it to yourself.

Feed your mind and soul with the power of those words.

Let me tell you, at first you may not believe it. Even the second, third or 100th time you may not believe it. But those words are the water and sunlight for the flowers of your beliefs that allow themselves to grow.

Repeat them. Repeat them when it's hard. Repeat them when its easy. Repeat them whenever you need a spark of hope and love. And know that you are the only gardener that has a key to your garden.

No matter what anyone or any other situation says about you – you are the only person who has access to the special food to water your garden. Only your words of disbelief or affirmation can allow those weeds or flowers to prosper. No – Matter – What – Anyone – Else – Says.

Now those weedy LSBs will still always exist, don't you worry – they are darn hard to get rid of. But they have a purpose.

They are there for balance, for humility, for our ego to not get too full of itself. But as long as we keep growing those beliefs with our thoughts, our affirmations or personal magic plant feed, that 1% inside ourselves that knows that we can be more than we are right now, may become 2%. Then that 2% may become 4% and, as long as we get to a spot where that percentage gets to fifty-one and has the majority voice in our head – we are on the path. The path to where we truly want to go and the path we know we deserve. Where we are worthy and where we are enough.

> You see, at the end of the day it is
> just a choice of words.
> Words that fuel us. Words that feed us.

So, if we take *away* that not it becomes:

> I am ~~not~~ enough.
> I am ~~not~~ worthy.
> I am ~~not~~ capable.
> Everything changes.

And those LIMITING self-beliefs become limit-LESS self-beliefs.

And without limits – anything is possible.

Even your most unlikely dreams.

Chapter 2

L - LOVE

"Let the beauty of what you love, be what you do"

– Rumi

▶ WHAT DO YOU LOVE?

Broad question, I know.

But truly, what do you love that you cannot touch, see or hold? What do you love that exists in no reflection in this world but only in the constraints of your mind?

Deep. I know. Let's back it up a little.

Love is at the basis of everything. Love is the reason we all exist. It is what we are all searching for in our lives and relationships. It is the reason that babies need physical contact to thrive and grow and the reason at our core we all need connection because we desire love to something or someone.

At the cornerstone of it all, love is the pinnacle that we need to target when we are wanting to achieve our dreams. Because, let me tell you, if you don't love it in any aspect, you won't succeed. Love is the secret sauce, the magic bean, the special ingredient that allows us to truly soar.

But before we get too deep into the love ocean, let's talk about success.

The nitty gritty, breaking-it-down definition of success.

We have gotten into a place in this world where success has been twisted, turned and distorted into this extra-terrestrial form where success = a number sign. And not just any number sign but a darn big one. The bigger the better.

We live in a society where we are forced to believe that a successful life is one where we have all the things bought by the big dollar sign assigned to our self-worth. That the more money we earn, the nice clothes we have, cool vacations we go on and latest technology we possess defines our level of success. If you are here reading this, you may already know the little secret that I am going to let you in on, but if you don't already know – I want to tell you that none of those things mean you are successful.

Success is a feeling.

A feeling that lasts inside of us even if one morning all of those things were gone. Where if we woke up one day, still with enough money to pay all our basic needs and get by without any stress, but we had all of the material stuff taken from us, we would still feel joyful.

It has been found that once all our basic needs are covered and our personal safety is assured – people's happiness does not increase when earning over **$60k - $75k per year.**

Because money doesn't equal happiness. Therefore, money doesn't equal success. At least in my definition.

Success = Fulfillment

Fulfillment comes from waking up being proud of who you are. Being proud of how you show up in this world. Being proud of how you treat others and yourself.

Fulfillment comes from knowing that you are being the best version of yourself in this lifetime. That is success. And that success – the one that we should all redefine for future generations comes back to the big L.

L O V E
The access to achieving that fulfillment is through love.

To get to that fulfillment, that success through the path of LOVE we need to find the G.A.P. inside of us.

The GAP is our Gifts. Abilities. Passions.

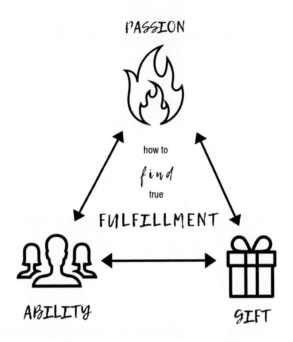

▶ GIFTS

Gifts are the things that we are born with inside of us. The little nuggets in each of us that we own. The talents that were wrapped up in a little bow and inserted inside our little souls when we descended on this earth.

But it is important to remember that we don't chose gifts, they are given to us. Sometimes we love those gifts and other times we don't. Sometimes we use those gifts and other times we don't.

▶ ABILITIES

Abilities exist in all of us equally. Well that's not completely true, abilities exist in the majority of us. The majority of us have the ability to walk. The ability to talk. The ability to learn and grow.

The ability to go and get a job. Make a friend. Cook a meal. Dance. Swim. Jump. Play.

The majority of us have those things in us. They are the building blocks. We aren't born with these, but we can activate them with a combination of:

DESIRE + ACTION

When we are babies, we combine the desire to crawl with the action to do it, then level up and walk. Then run. So on and so forth, you get the idea.

Abilities aren't anything special. They are just what is in the pot that makes up a human being on this planet.

▸ PASSIONS

Boy, oh boy, this is the part that I just frigging LOVE!

Passions are the real ooey-gooey, juicy and delicious fruits that shine inside all of us. The core spark inside of us that gives us the fuel to go after what we want. It is the stuff we do when we lose track of time and no matter how long or tired the activity has made us - we leave energized. We walk away rejuvenated, refreshed and craving for more.

It is the stuff that we would do even if we were not receiving much, or any, compensation for it because it just lights us up that much!

The exciting thing is that we can have more than one passion! We can have many, some that are stronger than others, some we would like to make a living off, others we just do for ourselves, because it makes us happy.

Not all of the things we love to do have to be our professions – sometimes they may be gifts, other times they may be passions.

GIFTS

- what you are naturally good at
- what comes easily to you
- what you don't have to work too hard at

ABILITIES

- what we are all able to do
- what exists in everyone when they try
- what is in the blueprint of humankind

PASSIONS

- what lights you up
- what excites you
- what sets your soul on fire

Are you a little bit confused? That's okay let me break it down for you.

▸ UNDERSTANDING YOUR GAP

When I was younger, like most little girls, my mum used to French-braid my hair. I loved it!

When I got to a certain age, I wanted my hair braided more often, so my mum told me that if I wanted to have my hair braided, I had to do it myself. She got out one of my American Girl dolls and showed me once how to do it. Within a couple tries on the doll and then on myself, I got it. Picked it up really easily, and with only a tiny bit of practice I became relatively good at braiding hair. Through my teenage years, I enjoyed doing hair, on myself and on my friends. Whenever we would have an occasion, they would ask me to either curl or braid their hair.

There were a few times that people said to me, "You should become a hair dresser!" I thought about it and truly it just didn't tickle my fancy. I enjoyed it a little bit, but the thought of doing that all day long with multiple people honestly stressed me out. I realized I would never want to make that my career or do it too often. Clearly, it was just one of my GIFTS.

This is an easier one to understand.

As you will come to know, I would like to say I am many things. Hardworking, passionate, a good cook, traveler and friend, not the most intelligent but I have a pretty good emotional intelligence – one thing I definitely am though – is being slightly idiotically silly at times. Some call it crazy, I like to call it hilarious. Through that zesty trait of mine – I have a few good stories. Because life is meant to be fun, hilarious, enjoyable and more than just striving for our dreams I want to break up the intensity of this book with a few little stories here and there to not only give you a little giggle break, but also remind you that I am human. I am stupid sometimes, I do ridiculous things and make mistakes. I am just like you. In honor of reminding us that we are all the same at the core – and what is possible for me is just as possible for you. In all aspects.

So, I am going to call these little story breaks –

"DKisms"

Lucky for us – this little DKism ties in perfectly with understanding the next part of our GAP - ABILITIES.

Before I ever picked up my life and moved to Australia, I was following the "traditional" route of going to university, because that is just what you are supposed to do out of high school, even if you have no idea what you want to do with your life. To increase my interest in university, I decided I was going to set the goal of going on an exchange – something that I could actually look forward to amongst the day-to-day classes. So, in 2013 (about 11 months before I got the opportunity to move to Australia), I picked up my life and moved to Copenhagen, Denmark. A country that was in Europe but still had a lot of English speakers.

Since I am a "goal setting" type of person and always desired to live a healthy life, I decided to set another goal while I was on exchange – run a half-marathon. Now before you go jumping to conclusions, know that I actually HATED running. Loathed it with a passion. But since all my older siblings had done half-marathons and I wanted to find some way to keep motivated to stay fit while on exchange – I decided that running was the way to do it.

Being a synchro swimmer my whole life, I was not and am not a land animal. For me running is awkward, hard and started out really not fun at all. I began with running a kilometer, working my way up to 21km by the time race day came along. I even actually started to like running… just a little bit.

Most of us who are able bodied have the ABILITY to run. For most of us actually doing it is the problem. Some people are naturally gifted at it and are just good runners without even trying, while others are wildly passionate about it and spend their life literally running about the world. Sometimes those abilities even turn into passions. That is not me. And that is okay! It just not my thing. It is someone else's.

Those are our **abilities**.

I trained for my half-marathon in Copenhagen which, if you don't know, is literally one of the flattest cities around. Not even joking you, the only hills that you encounter are on the bridges that go over the canals. So, training for a half-marathon in Copenhagen was actually great, because it was ALL flat! But the problem was, I was running the half-marathon in Gothenburg, a Swedish city a three-hour train ride from the Danish capital, and the route was majorly hilly.

When I left to take the train to Gothenburg on the day before the half-marathon, I packed in a rush. So, when I got to the city with my training buddy that afternoon, I realized that I had forgotten running pants! All I had were jeans, and I clearly couldn't run 21km in those. So, off to the shops we went to buy me some pants. Great, all ready to go.

The morning of the race I put on my snazzy new running pants, feeling quite fab and ready to smash this race out. I put one shoe on, amp-ing my mind up for what was to come then the other sho.... Oh no. I couldn't find my other shoe. I must have packed it, Right? Wrong.

I came to a half-marathon, in another country, on the other side of the world from my home and only brought One – Damn – Shoe. For goodness sake, DK!

The marathon was going to start relatively soon, and I didn't have time to run to the shops and back to be able to get to the race in time. So, I did the only thing I knew. Got all my stuff, put on my socks and walked out the door, onto the bus and straight to the same shops that I went to the previous day, to buy myself some running shoes. Walking down the street, on the bus and through the mall in my socks, I definitely got some funny looks. But I marched right on into that store – found the cheapest runners I could find (received the 21% off discount for all participants in the half-marathon that day) and went straight to the race!

No matter how jazzed up I felt in my whole new running outfit, nothing could have prepared me for that race! I hadn't run on a hill of any incline more than a foot bridge in months, so I felt like I was scaling bloody Mount Everest the whole time! Not only that, but good old Mother Nature decided to throw a spanner in the works with monsoon rain and gale-force winds during the race. I literally saw barrier fences being blown into the ocean while I was running! But – I made it out alive. Not only with another thing ticked off the bucket list, but also a brand new, wet and soggy pair of running pants and shoes.

I'll Take It As A Win. DKism

I hope it is all making a little bit more sense to you now.

Now, **passions**. This is where it gets really juicy. This is the stuff you don't have to be gifted at, but you bloody love anyway.

Now, you may think that I am just being humble, but truly I say – I'm not that good at synchro. Yes, I went to the Olympics and I worked really damn hard to get better to get there, but I am not a naturally talented synchro swimmer.

You see, for me it all started back in 2001, where my beautiful Mum signed me up for a synchro class one day. Being so far in age from my other siblings, like I said, I kind of grew up like an only child. So, to combat my Mum's fear of me being lonely, she signed me up for just about every activity out there. From tennis to gymnastics, swimming to softball, piano to ballet, the list goes on. Was I gifted at any of them? Definitely not. Did I have the ability to do all of them? For sure!

But since I didn't have a burning passion for any in particular my mum kept trying. I enjoyed being in the water but was a bit bored of lap swimming and honestly was not coordinated enough to go far in gymnastics – but I enjoyed them both. So, one day when my mum saw a local synchro class being offered, which seemed to be the perfect combination – off I went.

To be honest, at first I didn't like it. I mean it was okay, but my overwhelming shyness led to me not 'vibe-ing' that well with the other girls to begin with. But I stuck to my guns, listened to my Mum and followed through so that after a few years, I fell head-over-heels in love with the sport.

Synchronized swimming is an aesthetic sport that weaves together the grace and beauty of dance and ballet with the discipline and body-awareness of gymnastics, the teamwork components of rowing with the aerobic capacity of free-diving, the mental toughness of a fighter with the acrobatic capabilities of a diver – all wrapped up in a beautiful little bow with glitter, make up, music, smiles and 50% less oxygen than any other sport.

It is the most undervalued and over-criticized sport in the world. People's perceptions of synchro are still stuck in the mind frame of the 1930s films of Esther Williams prancing around in flower caps. What people don't see is the blood, sweat, tears, broken bones and concussions hidden behind synchro's beautiful aesthetic.

Audiences are fooled by the big bright smiles, which makes them believe that the skills come with ease, when really they come from years and thousands of hours of discipline, hard work, commitment and sacrifice. Synchronized swimming demands performance at a level that very few understand and even fewer achieve.

It is a realm that only the committed, hardworking and passionate accomplish from an understanding and desire to constantly push your mind past what your body thinks it is capable of. It is learning to disregard your lungs when they are screaming at you for oxygen and still surfacing with an ease and grace that can fool even the trained eye.

Synchronized swimming is a lifestyle, a state of mind and a way a being. And synchronized swimming was my first love.

DK's first bathers!

I was mesmerized by the older girls in my club, who could do all these amazing things, just with their bodies. They moved to the music so fluidly and walked around with such confidence. They were my idols, I wanted to be just like them. Not to mention when we got to competitions and pulled out our sparkling rhinestone suits, slapped on some lipstick and slicked back our hair with gel – I felt like I had found my stride.

I got it. I was hooked. But there was one main issue – I honestly just wasn't that good.

I am not really that flexible, I don't have the best posture, I don't have the ideal "banana" synchro legs, my big feet and massive toes are hard to point and make look dainty. My body isn't naturally long, lean and ballerina-like which is the "desirable" physique in synchro. I truly wasn't built to be a synchro swimmer, but my-oh-my, friends, I loved it.

One thing that I did have on my side was the ability to work hard. That ability is inside all of us, and I found a special way to harness it to my benefit. I had to, because I wasn't gifted. Things didn't come easily to me; they came with lots of hard work and effort. They struggled out of me through lots of repetition and frustration. But I kept trying, I always kept trying.

The passion I had for synchro, combined with my ability to work hard, helped me improve. By no means was I fantastic – but I improved. Slowly and steadily.

DK's first synchro team

Because you see, my beautiful friends – you don't need to be gifted at your passions. We all have the ability inside us to work hard and get better at what we love. And when you love something enough, when it is your passion, working hard doesn't feel as much like hard work because you love it. There will definitely be a few aspects of the hard work that aren't always fun, but remember the speedbumps we spoke about earlier? Yup. Just a little reminder, it isn't always going to be easy. That's okay! Don't worry – you are normal!

We are ALL capable of improving at our passions, even when we are not talented at them. We ALL have the capability inside us.

Because capability happens when we realize that we *Can Activate our Passions* and combine them with the abilities that exist in us all:

> CAP (Can Activate Passion)
>
> +
>
> Ability
>
> =
>
> Capability

That capability allowed my improvement to flow over the years, as I grew up through the sport. All the other sports I was enrolled in would come and go, but synchro stuck. It became my identity. Something that I proudly wore with honor when I claimed to my friends at school that I did - synchronized swimming.

That passion inside me also challenged and trigged my biggest limiting self-beliefs. Because, despite all this exercise I did growing up, my LSB of **not being enough** stuck with me and I used my vice to literally feed that limiting self-belief.

It wouldn't be until years later that I would recognize that vice for what it was and see it within its true form. Because I used my vice to hide my LSB for so many years, I never worked on it until later in life. I never saw it for what it truly was and nurtured it with love, affirmations and self-belief. So it held me back.

You see, because the weight that my body held on to was from me trying to protect and comfort myself from dealing with the truth of who I thought I was, which was not enough, never enough. Because I held onto that weight, I couldn't access my full potential while I was training throughout high school. And so it cycled – like it always does.

I didn't deal with my LSB – therefore I fed it with my vice – which held my back from believing I could pursue my passion – because I didn't deal with my LSB.

You see LSBs are SO important when we are speaking about our passions – because so many people don't pursue their passions because their LSBs take over their mind and manifest as FEAR.

Fear that we aren't going to be able to do it. We aren't going to be able to make it happen. Fear that it is too difficult, it will take too long, or it is too hard. Fear that there are already other people out there doing what we want to do, so we won't be good enough. Fear that our passion isn't worthy of a dream, because it isn't what everyone else is doing.

Let me tell you something friends. None of that is true.

Your PASSION MATTERS, your PURSUIT is WORTHY, and YOU are CAPABLE!

You know what happens to this LSB when it manifests into fear – it takes another form that we are used to, called EXCUSES.

LIMITING SELF-BELIEF → FEAR → EXCUSES

Because all of those things that I said before are just excuses. Excuses rooted in our limiting self-beliefs. But there always will be that tiny little quiet whisper of a voice inside us that knows we're capable when we **TAP** INTO OUR **P A S S I O N S**!

You know what is the most amazing thing of all? ALL of our passions matter! ALL of our passions are important. Not everyone has to be a writer, podcaster, speaker, "influencer" or "celebrity" to make a difference. If you love gardening and are the best gardener in your neighborhood that helps all of the community's greenery flourish. If that fills you up and brings you joy and makes you fulfilled – know that that is enough.

▶ THERE IS A POWER IN US ALL PURSUING OUR PASSIONS

I like to use my amazing friends as examples. One of my dear friends from high school, Natalie, gets seriously jazzed up by science. Me? I honestly couldn't care less. I know it is important for this world, but it just doesn't excite me. For Natalie though it does, and what excites her specifically is zooplankton … say what? I know, right. I didn't know much about them either. They are the tiny little microscopic animals that live everywhere in the Pacific North West Ocean and the salmon, along with other char-ismatic critters, rely on them as their fuel to stay alive. She spends her days studying, identifying and observing the patterns in the plankton comparing them to their environment and how the zooplankton could affect the other ocean critters. The salmon and other ocean critters need their plankton! And the plankton need someone like Natalie to care about them! That is her passion.

My other beautiful friend, Jessica, high school amiga, is lit up by helping people. She is studying to become an occupational therapist (OT), a career that is so varied and not many people understand. Basically, it is a diverse position that slots into so many fields where OTs help people live their most fulfilling lives – from people in geriatrics, rehab and children with autism to aiding in accessibility and universal design, mental health, stroke and traumatic brain injury, spinal cord injuries and those with neurodegenerative diseases (MS, Parkinson's, ALS). Jessica gets fired up by the ability to help people live their best lives! Would I want to do that? No, but I completely know that it is needed. I know that the world needs people like Jessica & Natalie. I know that this planet is heading in a better direction because of people like them.

There are so many examples – my beautiful friend Becky, who is a brand photographer and chooses to only work with small businesses or entrepreneurs who help other people, because that makes her soul shine. To another friend Erica, who works in retail and absolutely loves having the chance to make an impact on people's lives through enhancing their shopping experience by building up their self-belief in situations where so many feel self-conscious.

Think of the people in your life, or the people you have encountered who shine in their field. The field that they have chosen, based on their passions, because it is something that THEY love.

No way in the world would that be what you want to do – but you can see how happy it makes them.

- ◉ **Would you be one of those people who someone else thinks of right now? Are you pursuing your passion?**

- ◉ **If not, why not? What fear is holding you back?**

- ◉ **What limiting self-belief is that fear rooted in?**

- ◉ **What excuses are you making right now to not do it?**

Natalie, Jessica, Becky and Erica all have passions that expand further than just their career of choice. Like I said, we all do. There are other ways that they choose to let those other passions flow. Their career is just one of them.

We might spend a part of our life going after one of our passions and then another part going after another passion. Like I said – part of my life's passion that I pursued was synchro. But now I know my life is moving in a different direction. Synchro is moving to the side because the new area that sets my soul on fire is sharing my story, not for myself, but to inspire other people to live their passions and go after their dreams. Because I know that the more we ALL do that, the more this beautiful planet is going to flourish.

▶ TRICKLING IT THROUGH YOUR LIFE

You know what the beautiful thing about actually pursuing your passion is, though?

Just doing it is enough!

Throughout all my years of synchro, despite all the self-doubt and lack of self-belief. Despite my inner knowledge that I believed I could be more, but wasn't at that point, I know that I still loved it. And that was enough. When I got to Year 11 and 12 and knew that I was coming into my last couple years of the sport – I was sad, but satisfied.

I knew that synchro would always be part of my life moving forward in some aspect. Whether that be coaching, volunteering or judging. It would have its little trickle through my existence, because, beautiful friends, quite often when we have passions, they don't fully go away. Whether it be in a large capacity or a small one, keep those passions in your life, in some sense, because they are going to add to that little pot of fulfillment at the end of the day, which makes you joyful.

We all have multiple passions and can't give every single one of those passions 1000% but allow little bits to be in our lives.

My kindred spirit and divine partner Luka is passionate about coffee. He owned a coffee van in Canada, mastered the art of making coffee and even travelled to where the beans are from to get a 360o understanding of his business. For a while, he thought that would be his life's purpose – making the best coffee he could. But life adjusts for all of us, and the direction swayed down a different path, towards nutrition, food and spirituality. Has his love of coffee gone away? Definitely not! Whenever anyone comes over for a coffee at his place, he gets out the food scale, measures the beans, tests the water temperature to the exact degree and makes sure that cup he is serving is the best coffee anyone has had that month. Luka's coffee passion still exists inside him and he feeds his love of it still because it fulfils him, it makes him happy. But it's just not his life's purpose anymore.

You don't HAVE to spend your life's path pursuing your passion as your career. To be completely honest, you don't have to do anything. I am just here, as you friend to inspire you, fulfill you and uplift you to go after your dreams. But when this book is finished and tucked away in the cupboard, or given to a friend, you might let those LSBs reign in your mind again and push your passions to the side and do a job that you don't mind, but kind of sucks your soul dry. You may choose to take the sensible path. The path that society tells us we should go down, where we are successful because we have a "good job" and we "earn a good living." Where we can use the vice of consumption to buy all the things that we think will make us feel good. Go to the places on vacation that look great to our friends on social media. Do all the things supposedly "successful" people do.

Let me ask you this, though:

> **Does that definition of success leave you fulfilled?**

> **Does that make you truly, truly happy?**

Just think about that.

In 2010, after doing synchro for nine years, as a naive eighteen-year-old, I "retired" from my sport.

You're probably thinking…"Wait girl…what?! You retired at 18 – but how did you get to the Olympics? I'm confused." I know – we are getting there.

At that point in synchro within Canada there were really only two options for me. Try out for the National Team, for which you had to make the top 25 in the country, to then go through a trial process, be cut down to 12 athletes, and then be selected on the National Team, if there were any spots available. That just wasn't an option for me. Yes, of course, I could try, definitely, but I just wasn't that good.

My final year in synchro at Nationals, I think I may have just scraped into the top 100 athletes. Truly, for me at that time, that was enough! I never believed I would make anything of myself so that was okay! But as you can see, the likelihood of me making the national team was ever so slim. Highly unlikely. Extremely difficult, and I accepted defeat because for me it wasn't about being the best – it was just about being the best I could be, in the sport that I loved. And that was enough.

Now, this might be all well and good, to hear me talk all about passions, but you might have a big elephant-in-the-room question to ask me -

"DK, my friend – **What if I DON'T KNOW what I am passionate about?"**

First of all, my beautiful sunshine of a friend, I would like to say – "Thank you for being brave enough to ask that question." It is hard! Let me tell you that you are not the only one, don't even worry!

Second of all, I would like you to know that it is okay! Not all of us know, and for so many of us it changes!

Even if you DO know, but you want to narrow it down, here are a few questions to help you flush it out:

❯ **What do you know you are DEFINITELY NOT passionate about?** For some odd reason, as human beings, it can be easier for us to know what we DON'T want to do than to know what we DO want to do. For me, I never EVER want to be a mathematician. Power to them, we need them in this world, but for me nothing sounds less fun than sitting with numbers all day. Some other stuff that just ain't my jam – sitting in a dark room, when its sunny outside, being hungover, being by myself for too long, eating lots of deep-fried food, cleaning, packing.

❯ **What are some of your gifts? What comes easily to you? What do you actually enjoy?** Remember my little story about my talent/ability to do hair? Think of an area of your life that you haven't really had to try hard at. Think about if you love that enough to pursue it on the path to your dream.

❯ **This one is fun - ready? What makes you excited?** *List everything with no judgement at all. Every little thing that sparks TRUE excitement and happiness inside your chest.* So, for me cooking, making raw desserts and feeding people, travelling to a new place I've never been, painting with no time restriction or judgement, swimming in the ocean at sunset, learning about spirituality and all Woo-Woo-ness, hugging people, having long soulful chats, talking about the depths of people's lives, helping others find the spark inside of them, speaking on stage, sharing the fire inside me, writing and laughing a big bellyful laugh.

❯ **What are you curious about that you think you might like?** One of the most important ways to find what we love is BE CU-

RIOUS! Let yourself explore and adventure, and that doesn't have to mean travel. Try out a new restaurant. Listen to a podcast on something you've always wanted to learn about. Watch a YouTube video about something you don't know much about. Be brave to go to an event in your city about something you're interested in. There are so many ways now in this world to learn, create and find out about more things. The Internet has given us this beautiful power.

Now those are all powerful questions, but let me show you where the REAL magic happens.

Do you really want to be massive? Do you want to grab those dreams of yours by the balls and make them happy, to TRULY succeed? In the traditional sense and the fulfillment sense?

IDENTIFY your GAP – apply it to your life with **CLARIT**Y and you, my friend, will **THRIVE.**

Think of Usain Bolt, Michael Phelps, Elon Musk, Oprah Winfrey or Richard Branson. The big names. The hot diggity dogs of this world. Athletes, entrepreneurs and speakers. People who have identified their GAP. Because, you see, when we find the ability to figure out the **GIFTS** that we have, that we are **PASSIONATE** about, that is where...

▶ THE MAGIC HAPPENS

The magic of the universe takes in a big deep breath of excitement, because using the GAP and overcoming the speedbumps – my friend, you can only succeed. Succeed in our definition and in the worlds!

I went to the Olympic games and achieved an impossible dream, the pinnacle within synchronized swimming. Something I would never have thought possible, because I wasn't gifted at it. And that is okay! Because I have now found my area to thrive in this life. Through this. Right now. Sharing with you.

I am not going to be Michael Phelps, Usain Bolt, Oprah, Elon or Richard. I am going to be Danielle Kettlewell. A name you will remember, because I have combined my desire with action to activate my ability to speak, write, hug and love. I am so darn passionate about sharing this message with the world, to shed love and light onto the ones who may not feel it right now. And although the limiting self-belief that is in me likes to argue with my internal consciousness, I know I have been given the gift of my voice, message and ability to communicate love and inspiration with this world to inspire it to elevate our collective consciousness.

▶ IDENTIFYING WHAT YOU LOVE IS THE FIRST STEP

Doing it is the second. We can stop there, if that is fulfillment for you. Not everyone achieves fulfillment through going after their dreams!

But the **third step** – if you have a big dream attached to your passion – is to take the LEAP. Get ready to DIVE DEEP.

Accept the speedbumps, cycle through the steps to CLARITY and, most of all, be proud of stepping into fear.

The **fourth** magic bonus step to activating the mystic inside you comes from identifying that GAP and combining that with your dream. Then my friend – I can't wait to see the amazingness in you shine!

Still not convinced that you have it in you just yet? Don't worry, Sunshine, we will get there. In due time. Stay with me, and I'll show you how it is possible. And believe. Turn those limiting self-beliefs into limitless self-beliefs and realize that it IS possible.

Chapter 3

A – ADVERSITY

"Adversity is the mother of progress"

– Mahatma Gandhi

How you deal with adversity is all in your mindset.

You know when you are just going about your life, fine and dandy, everything seems to be going to plan, you don't have too many worries in the world, you're just minding your own business and then SMACK BANG DANG – you're hit in the face with some problem that definitely wasn't part of your plan, and now everything isn't going to follow course and it has screwed up your whole darn schedule.

Yah – welcome, mi amigos – this is our beautiful friend that we are allowing into our friendship tribe who challenges us, changes us and forces us to either level up or back down in our lives. This little sassy diva is called **Adversity.**

Let's be honest, she probably sits down and has a nice old chat with Mr. Who Am I? pretty often.

How often have you made a plan to go ahead and do something, anything! Whether that be a business plan, life plan, health and exercise plan – anything – and then SOMETHING happens that is not part of that perfect little step-by-step plan.

The hat drops, the brown stuff hits the fan, the direction gets misaligned and the perfect little course of our life swerves for a little while. The funny thing is, my friends, this ALWAYS happens, always. Adversity in some form, whether large or small, will always be part of our lives. But how often do we PLAN for it? How often do we happily welcome it into our lives and identify how it is happening FOR us, not TO us?

Not too often.

Now I am not saying that you want to constantly live your life looking around the corner and waiting for something bad to happen, that's not good either. You will notice that IF you do that, Adversity will find you more often than average, because she knows that you are looking for her.

Rather, we want to be in the mindset where we accept that this type of adversity **WILL** happen and make a decision about **HOW** we will deal with it. How we can use this situation to learn, to grow, to find out something new about ourselves that can help us move forward faster.

Because, you see, when adversity happens - we only have two choices – to back down, let it feed our limiting self-belief and douse the flame of passion inside us for what we love. OR we can face it head on – use it as fuel for the fire. As a learning tool to grow and a lesson to add to our little pocketbook, moving forward in life, to make sure we know how to handle it all better next time it comes around.

Yes, this adversity refers to our little speed bumps along the way – but this adversity is usually just coming in a more dominant format. The speedbump isn't just missing an important appointment because of traffic or having a day with no motivation. This is a lot bigger than that and it comes in two forms:

> 1. Signs for Learning.
> 2. Challenges for Growth.

▶ SIGNS FOR LEARNING

These are the kinder form of adversity. The kind that is really easy to see, with hindsight, but takes a little more practice when we are living in the moment. It takes a deeper level of self-awareness to be very honest with yourself and aligned with your GUT feeling.

You know that GUT feeling? Everyone has it. The feeling in the pit of your stomach or the lump in your throat that is niggling away at you. That is itching you to take a different path, make a different decision, or showing you that you are NOT where you were meant to be. It is not a good feeling. And the more we ignore it and allow it to go unacknowledged, the angrier and louder it gets. It festers inside us in a way that doesn't feel good at all. Whether that gut feeling be that you are not in the right job, relationship, friendship group, country or just on the right direction in your life. That gut feeling likes to be acknowledged, because our body doesn't like it sitting there. Our body doesn't like to not feel good - no one likes to not feel good. It sucks!

The tricky thing is that because of society, circumstances or our very dominant LSBs we try to negotiate with our gut, trick our intuition and deny the truth of how we feel because, quite usually – acknowledging that feeling is pushing us out of our comfort zone. It's forcing us to CHANGE and, damn straight, change can be hard.

That gut feeling will continue to tickle you, scratch at your insides and flip-flop in your tummy until you acknowledge it and make a change. And if you don't, that gut feeling will show up in your life through (you guessed it) **adversity.** It happens in little ways at first, if we don't listen, then bigger and bigger and bigger – to the point where an adversity BOULDER will WHACK us in the face and put us down and out for a little while.

In my own life, I didn't listen to the GUT feeling over and over and over again, so it grew to be a big darn freaking BOULDER that smacked me right off my path in 2013.

I never REALLY enjoyed school. I mean I guess most people don't, but the traditional institution of education was never an area where I *thrived*. I definitely worked hard and did okay – but it really was hard work. Not passionate work.

So, after I finished high school, I was not all that jazzed with my options moving forward. The school that I went to, the city that I was from, the family that I grew up in all showed me that going to university straight out of high school was the ONLY option. If you didn't, you were pretty much thought of as the dumb kid who had failed at life.

Now that is a massive over-exaggeration, and NOT what I believe in the LEAST. But there was the undertone in Vancouver, in our area that, if you weren't heading straight to university after grade twelve, then something was wrong. Therefore, I believed that too, so I saw it as the only path.

Considering that my parents had also worked so hard to put me in a good school and valued education I wanted to respect what they had worked for and their dream for me. Especially because both of them finished school in Australia in Year 10, with my Dad only to go on and get his GED in his twenties with four kids at home. So, as parents naturally do, they wanted better for me and my siblings.

So, in 2010, the year I thought I was hanging up my synchro bathers for good, I was also off to a new adventure to do "the right thing" and GO to university! Except, I had a few problems. Firstly, I just didn't care that much about university and secondly, I really had NO clue what I wanted to study! So, with lack of care, mounted on top of the LSB that I wasn't good enough to get into the major university in my city I found many, MANY excuses to not apply. And missed the deadline. I allowed my limiting self-belief to dominate my thoughts, manifest into fear and transform into excuses, with a result that PROVED my LSB right. I wasn't good enough. Good enough to apply or even make it in.

So, I found a small on-campus college that would allow me to transfer to the university that I thought I wanted to go to after a year.

I didn't like it. I had no idea what I wanted to do or where I wanted to go. I believed I could do something SO MUCH greater than what I could learn at University, but I was too afraid to go down a different path. And so, my limiting self-beliefs festered in the perfect environment to thrive – continuous self-doubt and self-hatred with a lack of passion. I had just left synchro, had a lack of direction and I had no idea who I was or how I was going to become the person that deep down I knew I could be.

I was in university, not enjoying what I was doing, and therefore not doing well at it, because I wasn't fully following my passion. I had other passions that I was weaving through my life to uplift me where I could. I was coaching synchro to stay in and give back to the community. I set other goals to travel because that made me excited. I worked multiple jobs so I could afford to go and volunteer in South Africa, then saved up again to compete at World Master's synchro championships in Italy the following year, then took out a big student line of credit so that I could go on a Student Exchange in Denmark in the beginning of 2013.

But despite all that insertion of passion through other avenues, I had a feeling that the path that I was going down wasn't right. It wasn't my path. A gut feeling in my core.

I was three years into my university degree, though, and had already been to three institutions and changed my major three times − I couldn't stop now -I was already on the path!

I was scared to go out of my comfort zone into the unknown. No matter how many gut feelings and small signs I got throughout the years.

You see, my friends, sassy little Adversity can be a little bit forgiving at first. She has a kind side. She likes to nudge you here and there to let you know that maaayybbeee, you should redirect yourself. She wants to give you the benefit of the doubt that you will listen. Adversity is sweet, but she is a bloody firecracker at her core. After she gives you a few signs, even more than a few signs − she will SMACK you straight in the face so that you listen.

Sometimes she has a little chat with All Knowing Fate and the Magical Universe to double check that that smack is needed to redirect you, because, CLEARLY, you weren't listening. Or sometimes she will smack you with a **Challenge for Growth,** so you REALLY have to sit down and have a hard think about what you are doing.

A few weeks before my big SMACK happened I wrote down one day that I was *bored with life.* How sad, hey? Of course, there are more sad things in the world, but me let me tell you, beautiful people, life is an excitingly beautiful magic pudding when we choose to see it that way. So, if you ever feel bored with life – that may be Adversity giving you a little tickle.

Just make sure you...

▸ LISTEN

October 23rd, 2013

I was in my third year of university, studying art history. Fascinating, but not the most useful knowledge for this world (no offence to art historians). I had completed a long day of classes, finished working at my cousin's fitness studio and was heading to training with my masters team. That lit me up!

Even though practice was from eight until ten on a Wednesday evening and I had a midterm that I hadn't studied for the next day, I always loved heading to training and seeing my friends/teammates. I had set another goal for the year which was to go to World Masters again which was in Montreal the following July. I was excited to have something to look forward to outside of school and accomplish it with some of my great friends.

We got in and did our usual warm up training in the dark old university pool. We worked through a few technical skills and went on to experimenting with some highlights! One of my favorite aspects of synchro.

Highlights are one of the most magical parts of synchronized swimming, in my opinion. It is where athletes defy the laws of gravity and use body strength to explode teammates out of the water.

Basically teams form human pyramids under the water with an acrobat at the top of the stack, eggbeater up to the surface forming a human spring as the acrobat leaps out of the water from the force created and flips in the air. Highlights are pretty spectacular on their own, but the true power of them comes when they are speckled through routines, when synchro swimmers perform the feat holding their breath to the point of absolute exhaustion and continue in the blink of an eye back to conducting the movements of the routine. They are spectacular, and they are one of the many reasons why I know that my sport deserves more credit.

Always being the bigger girl on my team, I knew that highlights were something I could thrive at. I was big, and I was powerful, and I could use that power to help my teammates fly. Literally. So, I always loved training highlights.

That evening, we were just trying a basic one. A tripod. Where two girls held my feet while another girl stood on my shoulders to perform the move. Just a simple little move that I have done hundreds of times, but this time it went wrong.

My teammate went up as her feet slipped off my shoulders and came smack down straight on my head.

Initially I felt okay, just shocked as I didn't see it coming. During the moment of darkness trying to comprehend what happened to me, my teammates pulled me up from under the water to take a big breath in. I honestly thought it was nothing.

But, as the evening went on, and the nausea in my stomach grew, coupled with pain behind my eye and a splitting headache – I had a feeling something was wrong.

I went home to attempt to study for my midterm the following day and, as I pulled out my material, I realized that I couldn't read the words on the page. I knew it was English and I knew it was the right material – but nothing made sense to me. Talking was so hard as I tried to explain to my parents what was going on. I knew what I wanted to say, but it was so hard to get the words to come out of my mouth.

The next day, after a doctor's visit, I was diagnosed with a concussion.

I was told I need to rest for a week – no computers, no phone, no exercise, no driving, no reading, no alcohol, no TV, no bright lights, minimal stimulation – maximum rest. God darn it that was hard!

That was my MASSIVE smack in the face by Adversity. I believe now, looking back, that I definitely wasn't on the right path. I knew it, the universe knew, fate knew the real plan, so they all worked together to make SOMETHING happen to detour me. And because I didn't listen to the niggle over and over and over again, I got a massive SMACK

- a CHALLENGE for GROWTH.

▶ CHALLENGES FOR GROWTH

These guys are the big kahunas, they come in two forms:

> 1. Build-Up of Denial.
> 2. Random.

▶ BUILD-UP OF DENIAL

The build-up from choosing to ignore all the signs along the way. The spicy beasts that like to put a massive spanner in the works and cause BIG pain, because we didn't listen. So, this is the only thing that makes it work.

These challenges can come from a build-up of missing the nudges, ignoring the gut feelings and denying the truth that is inside of us

These hurt. They sting really badly, and they are so hard. That is what happened to me and has happened to me many times before, because I chose not to listen to my gut feelings all along.

▶ RANDOM

They can be massive. Painful and extremely real.

Cancer. Unexpected death. Terminal Illness. Natural Disasters. The surprise ending of a relationship. Painful circumstances created to hurt you.

We all have them in varying degrees in our own lives. And, like I said before, the weight of pain, just like the weight of limiting self-belief is always equal. No one's is more or less important than anyone else's, because we can't compare. It hurts us deeply. No matter the circumstance, no matter the situation, no matter the severity. It is okay to feel that pain.

Know that this Challenge for Growth is happening to make us feel that pain because maybe we haven't allowed ourselves to feel that pain for years. We pushed it down. Denied it. Pretended that it didn't exist. So it is all going to come OOOZING out when this challenge hits us.

But we are always given a choice – because the magical Universe is beautiful in allowing us to have free will.

We can shake our fists at the world in anger, have so much darkness inside us from allowing that anger to fester and ask…

> "Why is this happening TO me?"

Which many of us do. Which I did, too.

When I wasn't recovering from my concussion as fast as I had hoped. I eventually had to drop out of the semester at Uni, stop all my jobs and allow my only "job" to be recovering – by myself, at home, alone, all day, with a fear of going outside because my concussed brain couldn't comprehend the world. I sat there in the evenings, called my friends after days of hollowing loneliness and boredom asking them, through the sobs, *"Why is this happening to me?!"* But what I didn't know then, which I do know now, is that that beautifully painful situation, that challenge, was happening FOR me.

If I could have changed my perspective and my question, allowed a little bit more patience, understanding and compassion – I should have asked...

▶ "WHY IS THIS HAPPENING FOR ME?"

❯ **What are the situations in your life that have happened and smacked you in the face?**

❯ **When did you feel the niggling gut feeling inside you along the way?**

❯ **Looking back now, do you know how that situation happened for you?**

It is okay if you don't know yet. The cool thing is that I PROMISE you, at some point you will understand. It might hit you one day randomly as this massive Oprah-like "AH-HA" moment.

At first, when we are just starting out learning how to deal with this adversity, it is going to be hard. Adversity is always hard, to be honest. At first we aren't going to have the tools, knowledge or experience to be able to deal with this adversity. We are going to shake our fists at the world, let the tears flow from our eyes and the anger fester in our hearts. That is okay. We all have those moments.

A few weeks into my concussion, when I felt I couldn't see any light at the end of the tunnel, I realized that I had completely lost the shine that I knew was inside me. It was gone.

There were no answers in the medical community. Everyone was telling me to do something different and I was so confused. There were no tests I could take, no scans that could be done to see my progress. It was all in my mind. I had no cuts, scars, bleeding or stitches. We couldn't put a cast on or give me medication to recover. All I had to do was sleep as much as possible and not do anything. And with each continued day of rest I felt my soul, my purpose, my light slipping away. Because you see I stopped doing everything I was passionate about. Everything that lit me up was taken away. That is why integrating your passions through your life is so essential.

No one could tell me how long I would be concussed for, or when I could really go back to normal living. I kept pushing and pushing to go back to my life, but when I pushed too hard the headaches would come back. The dizziness would confuse me, and the world would overwhelm me.

You don't realize how many visual stimuli our brains take in every single day until that noggin of ours finds it hard to process it all. There were so many variables, options, stimuli in the world outside my house, it was just easier to stay inside – but then the loneliness and isolation was deafening.

I am fortunate to not have depression, but I know I was depressed for a period of that time. A side effect of concussion. Not because I felt overwhelmingly sad about the situation, but because eventually I felt nothing. No sadness or grief, just emptiness and darkness. There was no solution to help. No straight answer to fix it. Not one doctor who could guide me. Just me and my brain.

I know my situation wasn't that bad. I know there are people who have gone through worse, struggled more, felt deeper pain and darker depression. In no way, shape or form am I trying to lessen the severity of anyone's adversity and struggle.

Remember what I said about pain though? To each of us it feels equal.

With hindsight, I honestly wish I'd had more gratitude. Focused on all the beautiful things in my life that I did have, as opposed to focusing on all the things I didn't. I spent too much time feeling sorry for myself and not enough time looking for the beauty in the situation. But we all have those moments in life where we are so stuck in our own HOLE of self-pity that it is hard to see the forest for the trees.

I now know this situation in my life was my massive **Challenge for Growth.**

Growth in my ability to self-reflect, growth in my ability to pull myself out of self-pity and growth to see that those situations are beautiful blessings, sprinkled throughout our life, when we choose to see them that way.

▶ ATTITUDE FOR GRATITUDE

Adversity thrives off of attitude. The attitude that we have before, during and after the actual time of adversity.

We only have two options – an attitude of **gratitude** or an attitude of **self-pity.**

The craziest part of it all, though, is that the attitude we have in the situation can determine the outcome. Adversity, at times, can be unavoidable and that is okay. But we need to choose our attitude when adversity happens, we need to think about whether we are going to use it as a benefit or as a deficit in our lives.

In the case of my concussion, I definitely saw it as a deficit in my life. As a reason to feel sorry for myself and wallow in self-pity at times. I tried to find my gratitude for the situation, but my negativity overwhelmed me. It ate up my shine and shadowed my light, because I let it. I let that limiting self-belief thrive in the darkness of that environment. Our LSBs loooovve to feed off the darkness of adversity, when we let them. But we HAVE to stand firm. Not let our LSBs overtake our shine. Defeat them with love and affirmations. Conquer them with our light, not our darkness.

It takes practice, I know, but, my beautiful friend, I believe in you.

Think of a time in your life when you had adversity:

❯ **With hindsight now, do you see the Signs for Learning along the way?**

❯ **If it came to a massive boulder smacking you in the face with Challenges for Growth, what attitude did you have moving through it?**

❯ **Looking back now, can you see what you learned from that situation? Can you see the beauty in what it taught you/gave you/gifted you?**

Now a little lol break amongst all this seriousness for a DKism

Do you ever have those situations that just make you annoyed? You don't quite know what it actually is, but for some reason when you do that thing, it just makes you a little bit...irked. Your eye twitches and a little part of you wants to poke a small dog in the face out of frustration. Well that's me with shopping centers and parking lots on busy days. It tests me, seriously bloody tests me.

This one particular day I got the perfect storm. I had a limited amount of time on my hands to run an errand and to grab something from the shopping center. It was the weekend, in the middle of a rainy day in Perth. For anyone who doesn't know Perth, let me give you a little insight. It is a beautiful city where a laid back and chilled vibe breathes its way through the city when the sun is shining, which is about nine months of the year. The immaculate weather means the city is built around constant outdoor living.. But there is one issue.

Every year, winter comes. It's almost like it surprises people. Seasons and a cyclical yearly calendar are not NEW, people. There has been winter every year for the past – how many years?! You get the gist.

If you are not from Australia you may be chuckling at me, because for some reason the world thinks it is only ever sunny down under. For the most part you are right. But nevertheless we do have winter. And in winter it rains.

The issue with that is that the whole darn city of Perth is made for outdoor living so, when winter does come around - every year, there really isn't too much to do when it rains. So the people of Perth flock to the mall and the movies.

This is my roundabout way of saying – there was a buttload of people at the mall this particular day. Not only that, but I couldn't find what I was looking for on my shopping journey. Therefore that 'wanting to poke a small dog' feeling was quickly escalating.

On my way out of the car park my anxiety was really pinging. I am stopped, waiting behind two cars waiting at a stop sign for their moment to turn. There were cars everywhere. Lots of traffic and all I wanted to do was get the heck out of there with my blood pressure level intact and without scratching any cars. I know I am already annoyed but these cars in front of me are really taking their darn time to find their moment to turn. I start guiding myself through a few deep breaths as I try to maintain calmness while cars start lining up behind me. I become that crazy person speaking aloud telling myself that this is all a beautiful learning lessons in patience, but not truly believing it. Five minutes go by. Ten. Then almost fifteen. Why won't these cars in front of me frigging MOVE!?

The steam of frustration is just about to start bursting out of my ears and my eyes are welling in tears from just wanting to get the HECK out of this parking lot when a gentlemen walks up to my car and taps on the window. Taking a deep breath, I roll it down.

"Um, excuse me miss... the cars in front of you are parked."

Yup. I was sitting there like an idiot – getting worked in a fury from the lack of movement in the two parked cars in front of me.

I could've had a little bit more of an attitude for gratitude in this situation – Dkism!

▶ BRILLIANCE IN RESILIENCE

The craziest thing is that the more we have an attitude for gratitude through the adversity in our lives the more we will learn to become RESILIENT. And there is so much brilliance in resilience.

Resilience is a hot topic in the sporting world. In the lead-up to major competitions, like the World Championships and the

Olympic Games we had a marvelous team sports psych named Brian. He had been to about ten different Olympics as a sport psych and worked with many athletes, world champions and Olympic medalists. So Brian knew his stuff, and he taught us so much about resilience. The ability to take on the massive adversity that happens, take on those challenges for growth and use those situations in our lives to make us stronger and better for next time. Because there always will be more times. Like I said, adversity is sprinkled through our lives. Sometimes it's like someone accidentally opened the sprinkle shaker too much and all of a sudden a whole massive ton of adverse situations gets dumped on us. And other times we will be in such a flow state that even if there is a sprinkle of adversity here and there we will barely flinch and we will see the gift that it truly is.

This resilience will lead to, what our wonderful sports psych Brian liked to call:

Bounce-back-ability

We accept the adversity as it comes. Learn from it, and each time, learn to bounce back even faster, because we have chosen to learn and grow. We have chosen to see all those Signs for Learning along the way.

From the time that I first arrived in Australia until the end of 2015, the national team had a coach from Canada, Lisa. She would fly over every few weeks to coach training camps. I knew of her from growing up in the synchro world in Canada and knew of the tough reputation that followed her.

Lisa was a tiny little beast of a lady in her mid-fifties, with lean muscles accentuated by tanned leather skin. She spent her life as a contract coach, flying all over the world to work with different countries. She coached the Brazilian duet at the 2012 Olympics, worked with South American countries for years before that, coached with the Canadian team at the Sydney 2000 Games and established synchronized swimming in Malaysia for the Commonwealth Games back in the 90s. At that time, in 2015, she was exactly what Australia needed, a no-nonsense coach with years of experience and connections around the world of synchro. She was tough and laser-focused on the goal of getting the Australian team to the Olympic Games.

She had a beautiful heart, at her core. We all could see that when we went to her home city of Calgary for a training camp in 2014, where she had us over to her home for a home-cooked meal and did all our washing. But on the road to the Games she also got caught up in the mission. Lisa was so laser-focused that I believe she got so caught up in the outcome of the Olympics she forgot that we were people, not athletic machines. She started over-training us, making rash decisions to put us against each other and unintentionally played psychological games with us.

At the time it was hard. But she taught us resilience. Lisa threw us adversity left and right and we all got better at dealing with it. Whether it was a surprise workout that was extraordinarily difficult one day, to being switched spots in a routine or told that you are not swimming in the squad of eight anymore. It was challenging, it was tough, but she told us to fight back harder. We didn't have a moment to feel sorry for ourselves. We had to bounce back fast because that was the pace that our sport moved at. No matter if your body was sore or exhausted.

Of course, at times it was hard to have an attitude for gratitude. If you suddenly find out you are not going to be competing at the upcoming competition or being picked on one day, seemingly for no reason. But looking back, it made us learn to react quickly, move on fast and not spend too long ruminating on why something happened.

Adversity comes and goes as quickly as you allow it to, because, at its core, adversity is all about mindset.

When it comes, of course, it will be shocking. Probably because you haven't been listening to, seen or heard the Signs for Learning along the way. As human beings we are allowed to be shocked, feel hurt, pain, regret or sadness. It is okay, initially, to feel angry, frustrated or discouraged. These are all valid emotions that need to be given space to move and flow through us, so that they can pass and not resurface. At their core...

> ## Emotions = Energy in Motion

So, they need to be felt so they aren't stuffed into our subconscious and burst out of us one day through repressed emotion. This is still something that I am always working on and it has taken me years to realize.

It is just not healthy for us to ruminate on those feelings for long periods of time. We don't want to wallow in sadness, bathe in regret and shower ourselves in anger.

What we believe is what we become. Just like our trusty old good friends, our limiting self-beliefs. If we repeat to ourselves that we are not capable, not enough and not worthy, we will feel and be that way. If we continue to repeat to ourselves that we are angry, frustrated, sad or discouraged – we will live in that emotion.

That is why, what we believe we will achieve.

▶ ACHIEVE WHAT YOU BELIEVE

Back in the 1960's, a good ol' chap named Dr. Bruce Lipton made a phenomenal breakthrough in the realm of genetics.

I know, I know. I'm not a science person in the least so why am I talking about this?! Stay with me – this is fascinating. Dr. Lipton published a book called the "Biology of Belief" where he stated that, based on his research in genetics, we can literally affect our genes based on the environment. This means that our beliefs can change our outcome. That is why we need to believe to achieve. We need to feed our thoughts, mind and body positivity to move through a situation.

Now that can be a lot easier when we are in a good mood. When we are happy and things come easily it isn't that difficult, right? Then SMACK BANG DANG adversity comes along, and that positivity and optimism is a lot harder. But that is when we need it most! That is when Adversity is truly challenging our deeper strength to overcome what is difficult!

SO, the next time you are hit in the face with adversity:

1. **Allow yourself to feel the emotion attached to the situation to move through it;**

2. **Notice the brilliance in resilience, realizing what you are learning from the situation;**

3. **Try your hardest to be grateful for what the experience is teaching you; and**

4. **Remind yourself that adversity is all in mindset, so make sure what you *believe* is what you want to achieve.**

▶ THE BIG "O"

Nooo, I'm not talking about Oprah. I wish! Or, if your mind is in the gutter, I am not referring to that either, you slick rick. I am speaking about...

> Opportunity

There will always be points in our lives where we receive opportunities. Options. Chances. They can be on either end of the scale; Good or Bad.

If a stranger comes up to you at a party and offers you an unspecified pill. I'm going to put it out there and say that is probably a bad opportunity.

On the other hand, if you are at work and your shift supervisor can't make it in that day, so your manager asks you to step up into the role for the day, based on your great attitude...

Let's just say this is a good opportunity!

Opportunities are challenges, yes, put in a different form. Something to which we can either say 'yes' or 'no'. The options are black and white. It is night and day; you get the point? Many times though, our sneaking LSBs poke through and eat away at our self -confidence so that we don't even see those good opportunities as a chance to level up but rather, we see them as a terrifying possibility of failure. Many people don't see the opportunities in their lives because they're too scared to even recognize them for what they are.

The bad opportunities are a lot easier to recognize for their authentic truth. Because that is when our handy gut kicks on in with the weight in our stomach and a big fat 'NO' from our intuition.

Do I want to walk down a dark alley that looks unsafe with this stranger, while travelling alone in Morocco? No.

Do I to let me friend drive home when I can clearly see they've had too much to drink? No.

They aren't too hard to find answers for. However, the good opportunities or the positive ones seem to be a little bit different.

And let me tell you my friends, 99% of the time when we walk through adversity and get to the other side we conveniently find an Opportunity.

Obviously, these opportunities come in different shapes, sizes and scales. Some are small, some are larger. And the larger ones really get to us. WE hum and ha over them for days upon days. Deep down we know what we truly WANT to do but choosing the answer 'YES' pushes us WAY too far out of our comfort zone for our liking. Our LSBs manifest into fear which comes out as excuses and we say– 'NO'.

Because it's too scary.

That's what my LSB wanted to say to me when I got to opportunity to try out for the Australian Team – 'NO'. That was my very first thought – 'NO WAY'.

I call that one time in my life – the "Golden Opportunity."

Something that many wouldn't even recognize as an opportunity because it was so big and terrifyingly scary.

Somehow, on that day, after years of letting my LSB eat me alive, even though I had the whisper of my soul always wanting to peek through, that day I found the courage to disregard the bum hole of an LSB and let the whisper speak up.

Because I had two choices. A 'yes I want to try out for the Aussie National Team in hopes of making the Olympic Games' or a 'No way JOSE' and continue to live the life that I wasn't finding all that fulfilling at the moment.

What helped me with that situation was the way I chose to look at it. I chose to look at the situation as...

> ### What will I regret more?
> ### Trying?
> ### Or
> ### NOT trying
> ### because I was afraid?
>
> ### I would rather try and fail
> ### than always wonder
> ### 'What if?'

About a month into my concussion, I felt completely pitiful about myself. In a place of absolute loneliness, self-pity and deep sadness, I called my parents, pushing my dignity to the side and begging to go and spend time with them while I recovered.

Since I was born later in my parents' life, by the time I was in my late teens they were well into their retiree years. They started to escape to the warm weather more and more often, being Aussies who moved to Canada but didn't like the cold, so they called Mexico their second home. Right after I got my concussion, they headed down to Mexico to escape the cold weather for the season. So, I was left living alone. Which I usually loved! However, when you are completely house-bound and told to not do anything all day long – the loneliness was eating away at me. So, a few weeks in, when I felt like I had already completely swept my dignity away, I called them in desperation asking if I could join them in Mexico, just so I didn't have to be alone anymore.

I remember flying down to Puerto Vallarta, crying as I stared out the window, trying to not let the friendly couple beside me realize what was wrong. I felt pitiful, running to my parents at twenty years old, begging to stay with them because I was terrified of being alone anymore. I knew the power of my LSB, and deep down I was afraid of myself. Afraid that I would end up in the kitchen with the knife at my wrists again, allowing my LSB to completely eat me alive and negotiate with my mind that living wasn't necessary anymore. I didn't want that to happen, so I tucked my tail between my legs and ran to my parents.

I know my situation wasn't as bad as others, and that there are so many people worse off than me. But I think that was one of the hardest parts. The cocktail of self-pity, self-disgust and the guilt of feeling so lifeless, when so many people out there suffer more. That is what happens when we try to compare our pain, though, that dark little LSB tries to negotiate with us and trick us into feeling bad about feeling bad! Remember – **pain is equal**. There is no comparison. As much as I am not proud of my poor attitude at the time, I am glad that I allowed myself to feel all the emotions; that they had the ability to flow through me because …

The feeling is part of the healing.

I spent my 21st birthday in Mexico with my parents. It was a day where, being my goal-oriented self, I had planned to run my second half marathon with my two beautiful long-time friends. "Run twenty-one kilometers the day I turned twenty-one." It seemed like a perfect plan! But, as we know now, Adversity had her own idea for what my life was to look like at that point.

The day after my birthday was another uneventful day. I spent my day moving slowly, literally planning the day around when I could eat a pomegranate, because the complicated fruit would take me about an hour to finish when I pulled out each pit, one at a time. A time-consuming activity that I loved, so I could count down the hours to sleep again and tick off another day in the recovery book. But that day I had something exciting planned - Skype one of my best friends at the time, Cassie, to catch up for my birthday. I wasn't really supposed to have too much screen time, but I was bending my recovery rules a little bit to try to maintain my sanity.

Cassie and I had met through synchro, developing our initially beautiful friendship after I "retired." We were on the same wave length, both high-energy beings, enthusiastic about life. Cas went to school in Montreal, and I was in Vancouver so during the holidays and summer we would catch up as if no time had passed.

As we were chatting this particular evening, Cassie got a message. A message that made her stop speaking mid-sentence to read through and comprehend. Her gaze shifted downward then returned wide-eyed back to me. I knew this was not your average message.

Her former synchro coach in Vancouver, Julie, had moved to Australia with her husband a few years before. Julie started working with the synchro club in her new home of Perth and eventually became the Assistant Head coach of the National team. They were reforming their squad after a large portion of the team retired, following the London Olympics. Due to the small nature of the sport in Australia, they didn't have too many people in the talent pool. Julie, from years of coaching Cassie knew of her dual citizenship due to her Aussie father, combined with her childhood dream of wanting to go to the Olympics, so she reached out to her.

They were looking for some more people to come and try out for the Aussie National Team to work towards competing at the FINA World Championships in 2015 to qualify the country for the Rio Olympic Games in 2016. Julie asked Cassie if she was interested.

We were flabbergasted. This was crazy! I was so ecstatic I could hardly contain myself and Cassie was so shocked she was speechless. I started to jump up and down with my concussed brain knowing that this was an AMAZING opportunity for her! ONCE in a LIFETIME!

I didn't even consider myself at all. It didn't even enter my mind. But I have two Aussie parents, I do synchro, I have the possibility of getting Aussie Citizenship.

After discussing all the possibilities and outcomes for Cas, her shock grew into excitement. You could see she had another realization and her face brightened as she said to me –

"DK – you could do it to…"

"When one door closes, another opens;
but we often look so long and so regretfully
upon the closed door that we do not see
the one which has opened for us."

– Alexander Graham Bell

The door closing is adversity. The other door opening is opportunity. With adversity ALWAYS comes opportunity. There will always be a choice. There always will be another way to go, an option. A path to go down.

But, like Alexander Bell said, we often focus so much on the closing door that we don't see the opportunity for what it truly is. Amazing. A blessing in disguise.

But to see that, it is all about mindset. An open mind and an open heart.

For me, the moment that door creaked open with the "golden opportunity" was the moment the course of my life changed, forever.

Chapter 4

R – REQUIRED ACTION

"Even if you are on the right path,
you will get run over if you just sit there."

– Will Rogers

Sometimes the hardest part of going after our dreams is taking the first step and diving in head-first, not thinking of the possibility of what CAN happen.

None of this – our dreams, our passions, our pursuits – can ever happen unless we DO something about it. We can sit there, overcome our LSB, identify our passions, take hits of adversity left and right, but we are going to be in the same darn spot unless we take a massive LEAP of action.

The most integral part of action is the LEAP:

> ## L.E.A.P
> Lean into Fear,
> Expect to Work,
> Accept the Sacrifices, and apply
> Persistence.

▶ LEAN INTO FEAR

This is one of my favorite things to talk about, honestly and ironically, because so many people are AFRAID to dissect it and understand it at its core. Fear truly is a magical emotion. It is the invisible, yet MASSIVE blockage between who we are now and who we want to become. It is the test in this world to challenge most people to become who they believe they can be, but many people are too scared to even dip their toe into fear. Because it is scary, it is daunting. Why live in FEAR when we could live in COMFORT?

Bleh. Comfort! That cute little word that gives us a false sense of security and has such a positive connotation. It's associated with soft pillows, cozy couches, luxury beds and warm sweaters. There is nothing wrong with that – I mean, who likes sleeping in an uncomfortable bed or cuddling up on a rock-hard couch. I get it. BUT – comfort should only be used to describe THINGS not LIVES. When we start to think of our lives as comfortable or living in the comfort zone – that often leads to dissatisfaction, a lack of stimulation, a lack of excitement in our lives. If you want to live a "normal" life and exist in comfort, there is absolutely nothing wrong with that. It doesn't make you a bad person, but I know that if you are pursuing your dreams – they don't exist in the comfort zone. We all know the quote;

> "Life begins at the end of our comfort zone."

You know what hangs out on the edge of our comfort zone? FEAR. As soon as we creep to the edge of that cozy little bubble of the comfort zone, many of us encounter fear, find it too scary and decide to back off and hang out back on our cozy little La-Z-Boy.

NA-FRIGGING-UH my friends. NOT us. Not in the pursuit of our dreams. Not in the pursuit of our passions, because you can NOT achieve your dreams living in your current comfort zone. You are going to need to...

> STEP into FEAR

Because fear is just = **F**alse **E**vidence **A**ppearing **R**eal

That evidence that is created by our sneaking little limiting self-beliefs doing a fantastic job of blowing things out of proportion through worry - through projecting an idea that what we are afraid of is going to happen.

- **How often have you allowed your fear of some future situation to consume you?**
- **Have you sat there and thought about all the possible outcomes if you screw up?**

I definitely have. I am human.

But think about it – what does that projection of worry EVER bring you? Nothing. We cannot control the future. We can only control what we do right now. So why spend your 'right now' worrying about some future now, when quite often there is NOTHING you can do?

If you have times where those LSBs take over, the fear consumes you and the worry takes on a life of its own – take it back to something I learned from the amazing sports psych Brian:

Control the Control-ables

Figure out what it is, in this moment, that you can control. What you can change. Then try your best to let go of everything else, because in this moment, it will do NOTHING for you.

As soon as Cassie said; "DK… you could do it too!" my LSBs had a field day!

LSB: HA! That is hilarious. What a good joke. Little fat, unfit, DK trying out for the Aussie Team. Actual LOL – like THAT would ever happen.

DK's Whisper of belief: I know…but…it sounds amazing. It is an incredible opportunity. This stuff doesn't happen. This is once in a lifetime, I know it.

LSB: Yah, an incredible opportunity for someone ELSE. Some who can actually achieve it. Don't waste your breath. Stop embarrassing yourself by entertaining this thought.

DK's Whisper of Belief: But. But… what if? What if it is possible? I know it is crazy. But what if?

LSB: What if- what? You try. You try and fail! Okay let's just say that you DO try right? First of all, look at the state that you are in right now. Yah, you might be a bit thinner than when you were in high school, but you DO NOT have a synchro body. Also, um hello. Let's keep in mind. You ain't that good honey. Remember? You never got anywhere in Canada, why would you think you can get somewhere in another country. Thirdly, girl, you are in Canada…well Mexico…and a current university drop out with no money. What in the world makes you think you could fly all the way to frigging AUSTRALIA to make this happen? Way too impossible. Nah-UH. You're not doing it.

DK's Whisper of Belief: But what if there is a 10% chance I can do it. A 5% chance or, bloody hell, even a 1% chance. A 1% chance I can make a National Team and then the Olympics is worth a shot, isn't it? It's the OLYMPICS. It's the international sporting event that makes your soul swell with love because you adore it so much and have been obsessed with it your whole life. There is a 1% chance that you could be a part of that!

LSB: Right. You think you have a 1% chance. Pull your head in girl. You're sounding crazy.

DK's Whisper of Belief: Okay maybe I am crazy! What's the harm is just trying?! Just giving it a hot shot! Imagine sitting watching the Olympics in 2016 - wouldn't you rather know that your tried and FAILED than didn't try at all – and then wonder what if?! What would you rather live with – the regret of never trying and always wondering, or the trying and "failing"? But those don't even have to be the only options because there is the tiny, small, third possibility – that MAYBE I make it. MAYBE I am ENOUGH to make it. Just MAYBE – isn't it worth it, the bet on an impossible maybe, rather than live with an impossible no?

You see, sometimes fear is good. Sometimes it can drive us. When we choose to switch that fear around and imagine it as living with the fear of NOT doing something. NOT doing something that somewhere deep down inside us we know we want to try.

Our LSB's are strong and powerful but that whisper of belief inside of us is stronger when we choose to listen. I like to call that Whisper of Belief inside of us our...

SOUL

Our soul is the part of us that is deeper than our physical body in this earthly realm. Soul has nothing to do with religion, but more to do with the essence of who we are. The truth of who we are inside, when we strip back all the layers and masks that we choose to wear to protect us in this world.

We all wear layers. It is scary to walk around as our complete and true authentic selves in this world. Our soul is sensitive, because our soul is filled with love. The more we expose that beautifully raw essence of soul, the more possibility we have of being hurt, if we aren't surrounded by the right circumstances and people– but on the other hand – the more we allow our soul to walk around shining its truth – the more likely we are to attract, create and manifest what we TRULY desire.

Because my soul, my whisper of belief – truly desired to go for this crazy opportunity. The opportunity ignited a spark inside me. Inside a part of me that I thought had gone quiet through my concussion. I was scared that part of me had disappeared. But it reignited my belief in the possibility of this world and what it can hold when you believe, are passionate and act. As hard as it may be sometimes, it is harder in the long run to ignore our soul's desire, ignore the whisper of belief inside us and ignore what we know we truly want.

Often, we may start off only hearing a tiny whisper from our soul and only have a very small part of us believe that something is possible for us beyond fear. To grow that belief inside us, we must let our imagination run wild, but to really make it happen we must...

1. IMAGINE if we did do it.
2. DO it.

▶ CONFIDENCE

Fear quite often likes to disguise himself. He likes to go undercover and show up in our lives as a...

LACK of SELF–CONFIDENCE.

Oh my goodness, my beautiful friends, do I know how real that is! I lived for SO many years with dismal self-confidence. A lack of self-confidence, which comes from fear, which is rooted in those dangnabbit LSBs. Thank goodness all mighty I was plopped into the sport of synchronized swimming, though, because that taught me my own major lesson in confidence.

I always felt self-conscious. Existing in a body that you don't love, being in a sport where you live in bathers amplified that for me. But I had two choices – quit because I didn't want to have to perform in one of my most vulnerable states, in my bathers, in front of everyone – or suck it up and find the confidence inside me to keep doing the sport I loved. Luckily the first wasn't an option. So I had to overcome that struggle of self confidence..

> One of the many reasons I love synchronized swimming is the requirement for athletes to smile. Now it is something that is quite often made fun of in the sport, having the big-mouthed smiles plastered across our faces as we perform, but it taught me one of my most imperative skills that has led me to where I am today. A skill that has allowed me, someone who struggled with self-confidence for YEARS, to be able to compete on the world stage. Because I learned to

> **FAKE it till you MAKE it.**

In some parts of the motivational world this can be controversial. People don't want you to not be your authentic self and go around in the world being a fake. But to my mind, it isn't related to that at all!

It is about pretending you are as confident as you wish to be, in your moment of vulnerability, so that you can inch closer to being the person your soul desires you to become.

> You see, because when you watch synchro swimmers in the pool perform with pearly white grins splashed across their face, you don't realize how much they are dying in that moment. Synchronized swimming is darn HARD. Competing routines are a challenge. Athletes are swimming up and down the pool at a hundred miles a minute going upside-down, right-side-up while constantly moving their arms and legs, counting the music,

changing patterns, being in time with their teammates, all while holding their breath for half the time. When you see them surface in the middle of a routine all they want to do is gasp for air because their lungs are screaming for oxygen, their bodies are in extreme fatigue and their hearts are pumping out blood at about 180 beats per minute (for those who don't know – that is about the heart rate Usain Bolt would have at the end of a 100m sprint). In that moment, surfacing – they don't want to smile – but they are faking it, because watching someone perform a routine while they look like they might actually die of exhaustion isn't that enjoyable as a spectator sport. Synchro swimmers fake it till they make it. NO other sports have to perform their skills in that state. Go ahead and look at the faces of athletes on TV when they are kicking the ball or shooting the hoop. They are focused and determined, yet they look exhausted.

The craziest part of all that I have experience from all my years of doing synchro is – after a while, as you have that smile stretching from cheek to cheek, a small part of you starts to believe it is true. Our bodies and minds associate smiles with happiness, even if it can be forced. Those are the neuro patterns that we have created from years of smiling. After years of swimming now, I almost can't help but smile when I am swimming and my body is struggling. Not only because it has become a habit, but also because it makes it easier. It makes my body and brain think that I am liking what I am doing, despite how intensely hard it is. It may just be okay. It may just be enjoyable.

After my LSBs and soul had that little internal face-off in my mind when Cassie mentioned to me the possible "golden opportunity", I allowed my soul the possibility to run wild with imagination.

I imagined myself trying. Going to Australia, attending the first training camp, meeting all the girls and working towards it. And it got me excited. I imagined training every day to prepare for the camp, which was about six weeks from the day we got the message – and it made me more excited. I imagined the possibility of moving to Australia, training with the team while working to make it happen. And it got me even more excited. I imagined the teensy tiny possibility of me... little old pudgy, not enough, awkward, non-synchro bodied, unfit, inflexible me ... going to the Olympics. And the thought set of a BONFIRE in my heart.

I definitely didn't feel confident enough to make it happen. I KNEW that people would think I was crazy. But I had to at LEAST *TRY*. I couldn't imagine allowing myself to live with the regret of – what if? I didn't want to go to my death-bed wondering – what if I had just tried?

What is the worst that can happen? I don't make the team, and it hurts my ego, bruises my dignity and I come running back to Canada. Yah, that is a possibility but then AT LEAST I would be living with KNOWING. Because **living with knowing what we are capable of, when we give it our all, is always better than WONDERING what we are capable of if we don't.**

Did I have fear inside of me? 100%. A thousand percent! But the Fear of NOT – the fear of REGRET, was greater.

The belief that I had inside was small, but it was enough. It was enough for me to take the first step.

I spent a few hours letting the possibilities ruminate in my mind. I played out all the scenarios and built up the courage to declare it. I declared it to myself, but for it to be truly real, I had to declare it to the world.

I walked into my parents' room, with my legs shaking and my nerves knotted up in my stomach and word-vomited the entire opportunity to my parents. I didn't even feel confident enough to tell them. I felt sick in the stomach thinking that even they would think I was crazy. But I imagined myself as someone who was confident enough to say it, to walk in there and declare it to the world. My body was shaking, my stomach felt sick, but my heart was burning – once I was done explaining my entire conversation with Cassie I said,

"I wanna try and do this, I want to try and see if I can go to the Olympics."

▶ DECLARING IT TO THE WORLD

This world, this universe – requires us to be brave. To have courage. Not just in going after what we believe we can do, but actually DECLARING it. Declaring out loud, to yourself and others, so that what you are wanting to do is KNOWN. This is a massive part of action. And it is so heavily tied into fear. Because, for some reason – saying it out loud makes it real. It makes it bigger than the fantasy that we create in our head. And, more importantly, it makes us accountable to our word.

Saying out loud to others that I wanted to move to Australia and try to make the National synchro team and qualify for the Olympics was completely terrifying! Every time I tried to get the words out there would be a big lump of fear trying to force down my truth. Force down my truth and keep me from declaring what my soul wanted. Yes, saying it out loud IS scary. It is scary to imagine what people are going to think, how they are going to react and what they will say in response. But it is NEVER as scary as the image we build up in our own mind.

There may be some people who tear us down. People who laugh in our faces and think that us declaring our dreams is the silliest thing they have ever heard. But if we are true to the whisper inside us, coming from a place of passion, and aligned with our truth, then whatever anyone else says doesn't matter. Because we know it is our purpose, our passion and our dream.

When I walked in there and told my parents about what I wanted to do – first of all they were a little bit shocked. I mean fair enough. It really did come out of nowhere. One minute I am in my room sulking and a little bit later I come out all inspired saying that I want to go to the Olympics. I get it.

But then my parents were really hesitant. Bless their cotton socks, I love them to pieces. I am lucky that they have been tough on me but also believed in me. They are supportive and wanted me to be the best version of myself. But they are also my parents and want to protect me from getting hurt.

My dream was so big that it even scared them a little bit. It scared them to think about the possibility of me failing, hurting and coming running back. Quite often the people closest to us can be the most skeptical, cautious and "realistic" about our dreams because they love us and are trying to keep us from getting hurt. So they let their own fear take over and project it onto us.

Additionally, I learnt from my beautiful dad the power of our word. Being a self-made business man, he has learned to become very intentional about what he says. He will never say or agree to anything unless he KNOWS that he can follow through, because his word has value, his word is currency.

The stronger the value of that currency that is our word, the more we learn to reap the rewards from life through achieving what we believe, because we ONLY say what we mean. DO what we act upon and then CREATE what we know is possible. We create evidence through experience that we reap in the rewards through an accumulation of experiences coming true.

This is why we can't go declaring things left, right and upside-down without the intention of following through. There is importance in having INTENTION in our word. Making sure that our WORD has value. Not only to ourselves and to others, but to the world, because it is ALWAYS listening.

How often have you heard people that say they are always going to do things, plan something, go after something else and NEVER follow through. They get word-happy and have no problem saying anything... but, you learn to never trust them. You learn to never ask them to do the pertinent task that needs to be finished or rely on them when you need something done.

We need to be intentional with our word. Realize the value that it has in the creation of our dreams, but only when it is combined with targeted and intentional ACTION. We need to be clear with ourselves, our subconscious, others and the Universe. If we go saying all different sorts of things and never following through, the universe is going to be confused with understanding WHAT we TRULY want.

> DECLARATION + ACTION = Building Trust & Belief

❯ **What declaration are you going to make about your dream?**

❯ **Who are you going to tell, to keep you accountable?**

▶ ACCOUNTABILITY THROUGH DECLARATION

One of the biggest breakthroughs when you do declare what you truly want is the fact that, now it is out there in the world, you are going to be HELD to it. Others around you who witness your brave declarations are going to hold you accountable to your words to make SURE that they don't dilute in value. Well, hopefully. Hopefully the people around you will hold you accountable.

They may not sit you down weekly and ask where you are at for a check in, however they will know and periodically inquire – as friends and family do – and that accountability check in – either passively or actively will hold you to your word.

Say, for some reason, you don't have people around you interested in following you up on your declarations. Maybe they don't ask, inquire or wonder how you are doing. First of all, may I just say – maybe try to surround yourself with some loving and uplifting people. But more importantly, you will know through your declaration that they know what you want to do. So even if they don't actively hold you to your word – the power of the value of that statement exists within the universe. And your subconscious mind will either feed into that through the fulfillment of following through or the guilt, excuses and fear of not following through. Don't let Fear get the better of you and allow the latter to happen.

If I walked around declaring that I wanted to try to go to the Olympics but did NOTHING about it – the validity of my word would be completely diminished. That is why it is so IMPORTANT for declaration to be followed with the next step of your LEAP into action.

▶ EXPECT TO WORK

Quite often people who dilute their word don't follow through with any action, any work or any effort. This is a step with major resistance. It can sometimes be the hardest to start, but one of the easier ones to follow through with.

I often think about it as similar to going to the gym to workout. Sometimes the hardest part can just be getting your bum off the couch, into the car and THERE and starting. Once you start, the flow initiates and it becomes easier. For me working is easier – for me it is the fuel to my fire and the potency to my words. I love to follow through and prove the power of what I am saying – for me the declaration of my soul's truth is the hardest part of all.

After I told my parents and faced their skepticism, I was inspired to take action and make it happen. After feeling like I was living in emptiness, with no sense of purpose, I felt like this motivated me to find my stride again. And, as scary as it was to see, hear and know the hesitancy of my parents – it fueled me.

We have a choice with people's reactions. We can use them to feed our fears, our limiting self-beliefs and halt our desire to take inspired action, **OR** we can FEED our ego, the desire in us to prove people wrong.

Isn't it funny how sometimes in life we don't have the true desire to follow through on something hard unless we encounter resistance? External resistance from others not believing in us? Why is it that we are so much quicker to believe in ourselves ONLY when we are doubted by others? Why can't we find the fire within before we face doubt from others?

Nevertheless, as long as we face their disbelief with inspired internal belief – we know we are using the power of their words in the correct way.

Looking back, it is so funny to see how motivated I was, despite my confused sense of where exactly to head with my direction.

Those words; "DK maybe you could do it too…?" were the spark that lit the flame in my heart that grew into a bonfire of desire and a forest fire of passion. That fire, though, needed oxygen to grow, the oxygen is the work. The action following the declaration.

So, I went in, guns blazing.

I contacted Julie, the assistant National Team coach about my interest along with Cassie's. Within in a few days we had scheduled a call with her, finding out more information about the opportunity. She explained to us that, after the London Olympics, all but one member of the National Team had retired. For most of them 2012 was their second Olympics and they were at a point in their life where they wanted to move on. That, in addition to the fact that they didn't have the most positive experience at the games because of the coach's attitude.

It can unfortunately be a bit of a pattern in our sport, for coaches to push the limits of athletes beyond what may be humanly possible. The long hours, intensity of training and cut-throat nature means every coach, team and country wants to push the boundaries of the sport. Unfortunately, athletes' bodies and minds are at the forefront of changing that game and can come out harmed. Excellence in sport is walking the tightrope between extreme intensity for ultimate outcome and over-training, leading to athletes walking away exhausted and burnt out. But that, in sports, is how champions are created. The ones who can mentally survive and the ones that can't.

I dived head-first into figuring out how I could best recover from my concussion. Luckily, the rest in Mexico had truly forced me to relax and allowed my brain to heal. But nevertheless, I was still determined to conquer it and not let it conquer me. We found a reputable chiropractor in Puerto Vallarta who found out that my concussions had caused a few vertebrae in my spine to compress. Helping heal that, helped my headaches, which aided my depressed state and led to healing my concussion. I spoke with people in the synchro world who had dealt with concussion recovery before, with my older sister Genevieve (who is a nurse) facilitating the discussion on the phone. I was determined to get better. I knew I would. I had to. For me, all of a sudden, there was no other choice.

I truly believe that not only did my sudden improved recovery happen because I amp-ed up finding the best treatment and truly allowing myself to recover. But also, because I finally DECIDED I could. That it was possible for me and getting better became the only option. Just like adversity, my friends – what we believe, we achieve. So, I chose that belief of mine to be a positive one. To be one that empowered me.

It makes me laugh looking back, because I was so determined and a bit aimless in my desperation to suddenly make this dream a reality. I decided that I needed to spend every spare moment doing something synchro-related, so when I looked back one day I would know I had given it my absolute everything. So, in every spare moment I had, I was stretching or doing some synchro-related movements. Even if I was just waiting for my parents for a few minutes – I made sure to soak up every single moment of opportunity.

It was cute, I was determined, but a bit lost in my sense of direction.

*Mara, Jess and Erica at the airport saying goodbye to DK
when she moved to Australia*

▸ MAKE A PLAN

It was so important for me to make a PLAN. At first, I was like a little chicken running around with my head cut off. It's hilarious to look back now, but if you aren't shown the direction to go, you will just go in circles until you find the right way. I realized I couldn't do it alone. I needed help. I contacted a few coaches I knew in Vancouver, and they helped me figure out a training schedule for myself until I could jet off to Australia.

Such an important part of that plan IS asking for help. Whether that be from the people around you, people you look up to or EVEN just doing a bit of research and figuring out the best way for YOU to do it RIGHT!

Remember that the way someone else did it won't always be the right way for you – you will find your way. But listen to the people who have done it before, figure out what you like about what they did. What you don't like. And use all that knowledge to devise the right plan for you.

My plan was to slowly build myself back up to training as hard as I could, to prepare for a training camp in Perth, Australia, at the beginning of January 2014. That camp was an open call-out to anyone interested in trying out for the Aussie Team. It was terrifying, definitely, but Cassie and I declared it out-loud, put our names down for the camp and jetted off to Australia merely six weeks after Julie contacted us.

Were we crazy? Probably a little bit yes! Anyone who has done anything great has been thought of as crazy by some people – but we were passionate, determined and driven to see if this golden opportunity was really, maybe, a possibility.

Flying into Perth we had no idea what to expect! We were terrified that the other girls were going to be threatened by us and think that we were two crazy Canadian's coming to take their spot on the team. But we had to just step into their fear.

Have you ever had those bizarre yet exciting moments when you meet someone for the first time that you just know you are going to spend lots of time together and become friends? Perhaps at work, or on a new team. I remember the first day we met all the other girls who later became my teammates, best friends and synchro soul sisters who experienced the crazy ride with us. We stood across from each other, introducing ourselves, awkwardly intimidating but also knowing we were all about to become friends.

The training camp ahead of us was intense. After spending the last few years not really training at my full capacity, because I thought the synchro chapter of my life was finished, my body was shocked at suddenly being thrown into **real** synchro training.

The camp was almost three weeks long, consisting of eight to nine to ten-hour days! Six hours a day in the water and two to three hours on land. We spent our days training under the hot Australian forty-degree sun, which was a shock to the system, coming from our skin being constantly covered up for the Canadian Winter. My skin experienced a whole new level of what it is really like to tan. I even developed a blister on my shoulder from the sun. But above all, the shock of how much I truly sucked hit me the hardest.

I knew going into the camp that I wasn't at my fittest. I knew I had my downfalls and I feared that my body, which was not the typical lean synchro body, would hold me back. But it was a real wake-up call to see how much I truly needed to improve. Luckily, I had never been the best on a team, I was used to being at the bottom of the ladder. So that part was normal for me, but it was still hard to bear. I let the parts of me that could shine – my work ethic, my attitude, my ability to work with a team. Non-physical aspects that I could control.

I needed that to shine through because I felt like I didn't have much else.

Despite everything, having my ego bruised and my pride a little hurt due to my ability, a spark inside of me still flickered. The spark of hope that saw the dream. That could grasp the power of possibility. Even though I wasn't the best, I knew I could improve. I knew, with a plan and in the right environment, giving it my ALL, I COULD get better. I was one of sixteen girls vying to be on the team. The National team. The team that was heading to qualify for the Olympics. They were only taking 12 and only eight swam in the pool at the competition, but I liked my odds. In comparison to Canada and so many other countries in the world – I was so close! I wasn't one of two hundred girls like in Canada. Or one among thousands like in Russia. I was one in 16 girls, trying to make the top eight. And that was freaking worth a shot.

I flew back to Canada from that camp inspired. My brain was racing with all the possibilities, with what I had to do to make it happen. I had to get to work.

That training camp was the beginning of the Rio Olympic campaign. Two months later, in Canberra at the Australian Institute of Sport, they were going to have trials. Then they were heading to Canada for a competition to prepare for a major competition, the World Cup, at the end of the year.

I had to:

- ❯ train hard to improve to be good enough to make the team;

- ❯ get my Aussie citizenship sorted; and

- ❯ move to Australia.

Of course, I wanted to make it to the Olympics. That was the end goal. But if I spent every day going to training and only thinking about THAT, I would never get there. I had to figure out the steps, the plan. Take one step at a time, keep my head down on the work – and only when I lost sight or needed inspiration remember to look up at what was guiding me.

It is so easy for us to get tied up in the finish line. Which is fair enough, because it makes us excited. It helps push us. It inspires us to dream. But quite often, if we ONLY spend our time looking for the end goal, we WILL get distracted, trip and cause ourselves to fall. Yes that fall may just be another part of our lessons in adversity, but it is also a reminder to us to stay focused.

If I had ONLY gone down my path, thinking about the Olympic games, disregarding everything else, I know that I would never have gotten there. Because I wouldn't have been focused on the process and the steps of ACTION to make it happen. Not only do those small steps keep us focused and in the direction of where we want to head – but also they keep us from getting discouraged. The process can be so extremely discouraging! Because the journey is so long, the road is treacherous and the task at hand is so huge.

I am not perfect, my friends, I screw up all the time and sometimes I suck at taking my own advice. Sometimes what I have to say is what I need most to hear and what I need to listen to the very most.

There were times on my journey when I remember coming home and crying to my partner at the time, Lexi, utterly exhausted and overwhelmed at the task ahead. I lost sight of the joy of the day-to-day and could only see the epic marathon of work that I had ahead of me. My body was exhausted, my mind was fatigued, my heart ached from missing my family and the impossibility of it all swallowed me whole.

That is okay. We all have those moments. We are allowed to feel that way. In the pursuit of your dreams, the journey is long and often seems near-impossible. The "goal" at the end of the day can seem so entirely far away that we almost want to just GIVE UP trying because "What is the point?"! But remember, my beautiful friends. Just take One - Step - At - A - Time.

Isn't it is funny how we are as human beings? We get frustrated when we go through difficult times, but then we suck it up. Trek through it. And think we are back on the path of least resistance until BOOM! It happens again. Because – life.

After I had recovered from my concussion and returned from the first training camp in Australia, I thought I was ready to rumble. Set to go. Guns blazing, ready to attack the one shot I had and make the most of it. I was blazing straight ahead to success! I was working hard again. Balancing working with and trying to get my head back into Uni. Six weeks went by and I had to head back to Australia for the National Team trials.

I wasn't able to move to Australia at that point because I was still sorting through the technicalities of my citizenship. I had the right to Aussie citizenship by descent, due to my parents being from Sydney, but I was working my way through the application process – which, with government issues, we all know can sometimes take a while.

I worked hard. I was proud of doing it all alone. I was proud of my drive and my commitment. I was ready to show the coaches my improvement and that I was someone who they wanted on their team.

I arrived in Canberra, being more familiar now with all the girls. Stoked to go into my first training session. Ready to show everyone what I was made of.

We were doing highlights first – GREAT! My strength! First highlight – let's go!

BANG!

Yup.

First highlight, first hour of training on the first day – I got another concussion.

Good old adversity, always loves to sneak up on us and chuck us a challenge when we least expect it, when we think we've got it all together. This piece of adversity for me was a beautiful learning lesson. I was being tested. Tested to see if I had learnt from the last one. Tested to see if I had the drive and desire inside me to actually go for it, to not be scared and intimidated by the fear.

Sometimes amongst all this adversity it can get a little tense – so why not take a moment for a quick little DKism breather.

In the process of writing this book I obviously spent many hours on the computer. I honestly really enjoyed every moment of the whole journey. My Friday nights and weekends were spent writing away instead of doing the "normal" things someone my age would do.

One Friday evening, when I was giving myself a break, I shut my laptop to go and watch the sunset. When I came back home to get back into the groove, I pulled out my laptop, but had one small problem. I couldn't open it. I pulled and pulled, but it felt like it was locked shut! I thought that something must be stuck in it, jamming it from opening.

Trying not to panic I told myself that, "It's fine. It's just a sign that maybe I need to take the night off." I didn't want to force it open in the fear that I might snap the screen and lose everything - lose my whole book. So I did the most sensible thing I could in that moment, called up the Steve Jobs gods at the Apple store to book an appointment.

The next morning, I drive half an hour out of my way, hoping and praying that whatever the issue is, it isn't expensive. I get there, walk in and explain my issue to the Genius. Seeming as perplexed as me with the problem, he has a little look at the laptop and pulls out what looks like a letter opener. He shimmies it in between the two sides of the stuck laptop as I hold my breath.

One minute later, it miraculously opens! Relief washed over me and then utter embarrassment as I realized that the mysterious reason it was closed was not some bizarre issue. Nope. It was because there was sticky tac on the screen. Yup. It was not jammed but just literally stuck. Because genius DK over here put sticky tac on her screen the night before to cover the time.

"Well that's probably the easiest job I am going to do all day", the genius chuckles as I walk away with my tail between my legs feeling a bit like an imbecile.

Adversities in life com in many forms, and sometimes they just come our way to wake us laugh. DK-ism.

After my second concussion, I was ready to listen. I had learned so much of what to do and not do from my last concussion. As well, I was lucky enough to be in one of the best places to be recovering from a concussion – the Australian Institute of Sport.

Straight away I went to see a doctor, they tested me and sent me back to my room with the prognosis. My favorite – rest. Lots of it. No screens. No over-stimulation and also definitely no way was I getting fully back into the water for this training camp. My heart was shattered, because I was so keen to show off my hard work, to show everyone why I deserved to be there, but it just wasn't my time - yet.

Every day I went to see the doctor, did a few concussion tests – walked a line, balanced, did a card memory game, had my pupils checked, was reminded to rest and relax. Golly flipping gee I was frustrated – so frustrated that I had flown all the way to Canberra, Australia to get hit in the head and lay in bed for two weeks. But, like I said, I had learned and although I allowed a pinch of self-pity to sneak its way in, I had so much more gratitude in the situation.

I was so grateful that I had the experience the few months before and I knew what I should and shouldn't do. I knew that I shouldn't push myself too much, like I did before, because it would only make the headaches continue and postpone my recover. It taught me an ultimate lesson in self-discipline and balancing what I wanted to do with what I knew I should do.

I spent two weeks in Canberra at the AIS recovering. Little-by-little I was allowed to do more. I could do laps for ten minutes a day, twenty minutes, thirty, an hour. I practiced my hand-eye coordination, carrying around a tennis ball that I was meant to toss and catch whenever I could. I sat and observed my teammates, the trials, the camp and every moment sitting out of the water and watching them train for eight hours a day was like fuel to the fire inside of me. It reminded me HOW badly I wanted this. How ready I was to work for it and how willing I was to do whatever it took to get myself there.

I was lucky to get a medical exemption from the trials and, considering there were only twelve trying out and twelve making the squad – I was, at that point, part of the team.

I flew back to Canada with the plan to meet my teammates in Calgary (a one-hour flight from Vancouver) in a couple weeks for another training camp before we headed to the Canadian Open.

Hindsight is a beautiful thing.

With the hindsight that I gained from having gone through recovery from my first concussion, which took me about two months – within three weeks of my second one I was feeling better.

I wasn't physically where I wanted to be from a fitness point of view heading into our training camp in Calgary – however, I was ready to work. I was on the 12-man squad heading into the camp and I was determined to make it into the team of eight.

At the senior level of synchronized swimming, teams compete in two routines at competitions – a technical routine and a free routine.

For the technical routine every team must include the five main elements within the routine. Elements are technical moves in synchro that highlight the skill of the athletes. I often explain it as similar to skating, if you have ever had the chance to watch a skater do a triple Lutz or other moves. The rest of the routine is choreographed around the main elements. Judges give the teams a score for each element performed by the team, as well judging the overall difficulty and artistic impression of the routine.

Free routines are longer, and quite often the more interesting routines. There is complete free rein and the routine can consist of anything choreography-wise as long as there are eight athletes and it is within the time limit.

By the time I got to Calgary and started training with the team again I was feeling better. Not my best, but better! Good enough that I was put on the team of eight swimming in the senior free routine at the Canadian Open the following week!

Walking into the Canadian Open as part of the Australian Team was such a surreal experience. Not only did I walk away from that same competition four years earlier, thinking my time in the sport was done, but also I was there as part of a team that I never thought I would be a part of in my wildest dreams! And it was so bloody intimidating. Honestly, I not only felt like a traitor but also felt like a fraud.

As excited as I was about going down this path, I felt guilt. A niggling feeling of guilt that slowly was eating at me. That guilt was twofold. You see I had always been proud to have Australian heritage; I would proudly proclaim to anyone that my family was from Australia, feeling like I was a little part of being a true-blue Aussie too. But I was also so proud to be Canadian. I mean, I grew up there. I travelled around the world proudly having the maple leaf stamped on my bag. Proudly clarifying that I was from Canada and NOT the US when people would inquire about my accent.

So, going to the Canadian Open, as a proud Canadian being part of the Aussie team, technically competing against the country that I loved so much, was conflicting for me. We were competing against Team Canada who, only a few years earlier, I had patriotically cheered on at the London 2012 Olympics!

Also the limiting self-beliefs inside me ate me alive at MY ability to be on a National Team. I knew from experience how damn hard girls work in Canada to get on their National team and I seemed to just waltz straight onto the Aussie team. The Canadian team was at a much higher standard and, honestly, we couldn't really even be thought of as competition because we were in completely different judging categories, but that guilt was definitely there.

▶ GUILT

Sometimes when we start to go after our dreams, our goals, step into our fears and leap at opportunities no matter how much they scare us, we will face GUILT. Because we are doing something we love, when maybe we should be doing something "practical" or "realistic." Guilt that we are doing something that maybe we think SOMEONE ELSE deserves more than us.

These thoughts stem from our LSBs. Those little buggers, I know. They are at the CORE of everything! Because, AGAIN, they are trying to hold us back.

I felt guilty for the opportunity that I got that I know not everyone gets. MY parents, my privilege to get citizenship to Australia, opened the doors for me to have an opportunity that so many would do anything for.

I had a choice. We all have a choice!

All negative feelings are fuel. Fuel to a flame that we can foster into a bonfire of passion and love, if we choose to, or fuel that can douse the belief inside us. We can use those feelings to fuel our LSBs, which leads to self-sabotage, or we can use it as FUEL for our dreams.

I had a choice. I wanted this so bad. I wanted to be part of the team and have the teensy, weensy chance of getting to the Olympics SO bad, I didn't want to give it up because of guilt. So I decided to use it as fuel.

I decided to work my ass off, not just for me but for every girl in Canada who had that Olympic dream and might not make it because the chances were smaller, the same opportunity wasn't there. I decided to use that guilt to make it bigger than me. I decided that IF something were to come from all of this, IF I was to get to the Olympics, I would contribute – give back, share my journey, share my story. Help others and the synchro community in some way that would make it all worth it. Because I knew HOW hard it was. It's hard, damn hard, to get to an Olympic Games. So many people don't make it. So many people spend their lives trying but never get there. So it had to be bigger than me. So that is what I did.

Do you have guilt on your journey?

❯ **Where does it stem from?**

❯ **How are you going to choose to use that guilt as fuel?**

❯ **What will YOU do?**

We competed at the Canadian Open and honestly, we weren't that great. We were a new team, literally from all over the world, who had been whacked together and told to compete for Australia with little training together. We all knew we had a long way to go, a lot to work on. Was it hard going out there, giving it our all and knowing we had so far to go? Knowing that our best at that time wasn't enough? Definitely! It takes a moment where you have to sit there, swallow your pride and just DO IT!

You can prepare, prepare, prepare until the cows come home but unless we actually go out there and DO the THING. Compete. Start the business. Perform. Show Up. Speak. Make the invest-ment – nothing will happen. You won't be fully prepared at first. You will NEVER feel FULLY prepared at first, there will be fear, but you just have to (literally)...

LEAP

Part of that leaping and going for it involves a little bit of us swal-lowing our dignity. Our pride. Our ego that is just trying to protect us from screwing up. Because you will NOT be perfect the first time. You will NEVER be perfect. But you just have to do it.

Going out there at the Canadian Open, competing in front of not only my former coaches but also girls that I used to coach myself took a massive amount of swallowing my pride. I knew that I wasn't at my peak just yet. I wasn't were I wanted to be only four or five months in from beginning this crazy journey, but I had to just do it. Put in the hard yards, get the repetition in the book and brain and do it.

It wasn't our best, but it was a start. And that was good enough.

▶ SACRIFICES

Now this is a hard one. This separates those who are TRULY committed to the dream from those who are only wanting to keep that dream within the constraints of their imagination.

> **What are you willing to give up NOW to be able to have what you truly desire in the future?**

Some people don't like calling them sacrifices. Fair enough. Maybe that is too harsh for you. Maybe that sounds a bit too "Jesus-sacrificial-lamb" intense for you. Another way to think of it is...

> **ALIGNING your CHOICES with your dream.**

What decisions are you going to make in your life to continue on the path to lead you to your deepest desires? For me, I call them sacrifices because they are hard. They can be not doing something that you love because it doesn't align with your greater purpose. Sometimes it hurts. That is why it separates the committed from the uncommitted.

I had to make the sacrifice of my environment, my family, my comfort zone. My family and friends mean the absolute WORLD to me. I love them with all my heart and soul. But if I wanted to go for it, continue to be on the Aussie team and go to the Olympics, there was obviously no way that I could stay in Vancouver.

I had to move. I had to leap out of my comfort zone and move across the world. So that is what I did.

Leaving was heart wrenching. I was saying goodbye and I honestly didn't know when I was going to be back. If I was going to be back. It was a goodbye with an unknown ending.

Hindsight is a beautiful thing isn't it? What I realized is that going to Denmark on exchange in Copenhagen the previous year was the Universe prepping me. Letting me get used to what it would be like to be alone, without family or friends to rely on. It prepared me to miss all the birthdays, holidays and family get-togethers. I learned how to get used to the homesickness and how to deal with it when it arises. And I came to understand how to figure it out on my own. I didn't have anyone to fall back on. It was just me. So I could do that, I was ready for that.

One of the hardest things for me, was the sacrifice of being away from my nieces and nephews. At the time, they were all so little! There were about ten of them aged seven and under. I loved them with all my heart. I am such a proud Aunty. After I worked through that initial frustration as a four-year-old, I fell in love with being an Aunty. And when my second niece, Charlotte was born, ten years after my first niece Meleah – I vowed to be the best Aunty I could be in my lifetime.

So, leaving them with the knowledge I was walking away from watching them grow up tore me up inside. It made me feel GUILTY for being selfish. Putting my own desires before theirs.

But remember – we have a choice with that guilt. I chose to use that emotion – again – to fuel me. I decided that I wanted to love them by showing them. Showing them that it is possible. I want all of my nieces and nephews to go after their dreams, do what they love and, most of all, be happy. So I had to show them. I couldn't just tell them.

I wanted them to see that if their Aunty can go do it – they can too. Because they are the next generation. They are the gifted generation that will have the ability far beyond our own to TRULY change the world by changing THEIR world.

The handfuls of us doing it now, are just paving the way for them. We may be the odd ones. The outliers. But when they come along it will be normal.

I wanted to do it for me, but also do it for them. (aaannnddd maybe a little bit of me wanted to be the cool Aunty!)

The Kettlewell family at Christmas

Sacrifice #1 – Time - sacrificing that time with my family. That choice was to put myself before having a quantity of time with them. Instead I would just have to do my best and focus on quality time.

Sacrifice #2 – Environment – I couldn't be in my environmental comfort zone if I wanted to do something that challenged me to be out of my comfort zone.

When we are in pursuit of our dreams we have to take a HARD look at what surrounds us.

> **Is the environment we are existing in facilitating the dream we are working towards?**

If it isn't, change it. I know that may sound too simple or maybe it is harsh. I know. But remember, my friends, it isn't always supposed to be easy. If you want to prove to the world that you are serious about this, you need to show it. Now I am not saying that everybody needs to move countries and walk away from their family. It is about being AWARE of the environment you are existing in most of the time and knowing if that is supporting where you are heading.

Maybe your dream is to start your own business in health and fitness. Let's just say that you love and adore your family, but they aren't supportive of that dream. That is hard. My love and compassion go out to you. Don't cut off your family. Just be aware of the amount of time you spend with them discussing the pursuit of your dreams, discussing your progress. When you do speak about it, say it with the confidence that exists inside of you because you KNOW it is your truth. You know it is your purpose. And be aware that their thoughts and beliefs about what you are going to do don't become your own beliefs.

When we are in an environment that isn't supportive of what we are working towards it is easy for us to take on the beliefs of others. Others who are not dealing with their own Limiting Self-Beliefs of what they think is possible in their own life, so they project them onto you. Because remember, amigos,

> **What other people say about you is a reflection of how they FEEL about themselves, NOT how they feel about you.**

This is in both a positive and negative way. People who are happy, loving, caring and aware of their own struggles, demons and negative patterns that come out as limiting self-beliefs, most likely will shine down words of love and praise. People who are struggling within themselves to find self-love, self-acceptance and who are denying themselves the possibility of true fulfillment because of that, will try to tear you down, in a desperate attempt to make them feel better about themselves.

For me, that environment that I needed to be in was Australia. In a place that supported my goals of getting on the team. So therefore, I needed to be with the team.

So, in May of 2014, when I finally received my Aussie passport, I packed up my life into two suitcases, said a heart wrenching goodbye to all the ones I loved, and flew to Perth, Australia, a city that is literally one of the furthest places from Vancouver, Canada – but it was the environment I needed to be in. Julie, the assistant national team coach was based there along with a few other girls on the Aussie team and Cassie, who had moved a couple months prior to me. I barely knew a soul. I was scared. But I leaped.

From the moment I flew into Perth I had my eyes, heart and soul set on the goal. As much as I had fear inside me I also had so much determination. Because, when you make that sacrifice of what you are leaving behind and make a CHOICE to focus on the beauty and goodness that lies ahead of you, the fear will slowly slip away. As much as I knew I missed my family and friends, my life was in Australia now and I had to focus on that.

As we work on existing in the present moment of what WE are doing and not focusing on the past or the OTHER part of life that we are missing out on – that pain and heart wrench will slowly dissipate.

I flew into Perth and started training with my squad. We formed this beautiful little family of expats who were all pursuing a dream. Four of us moved to Perth to train with the club there and only one girl already called the city home.

Amie, a bubbly blonde ray of sunshine, moved from Sydney to Perth at only 17. Rose had picked up her life from Auckland, New Zealand and moved to Australia as well, in the pursuit of the same Olympic dream. Her only difficult caveat though was she didn't yet have Australian citizenship. Rose was one of the most gifted athletes in NZ, but she believed that Australia had a better chance of getting to Rio, so she hoped she could expedite her citizenship process living in Perth and get it in time to make it to the Games. Cas moved a couple months before me, because she already had her Aussie citizenship by descent and stayed with some of her Dad's family who were Perth natives. Debbie, the only one who didn't move, wasn't even Perth born and bred as her family had emigrated from Singapore to Perth five years previously.

We were all strangers, expats, synchro swimmers and suddenly teammates who slowly became each other's family. None of us, except Debbie, really had other friends or family to lean on – we just had each other. And that bonded us. We became each other's family.

Because I planted myself in the right environment, I started to soar. I was in the right place, training with my teammates who supported my goals, our goals. We pushed each other, supported each other. We would challenge each other daily, keep each other on our toes and pick one another up when we were down. We were a tribe. And together we soared.

I started to improve. Fast. Going from training on my own to training with a team, a coach and a plan allowed me to grow like a weed. Don't get me wrong. I worked hard. Damn hard. I had challenges; we all do. There were many things I sucked at, times I wanted to give up. But I just kept putting one foot in front of the other, with my eyes focused on the path in front of me and my heart set on the light at the end.

It took discipline and commitment. That is where the environment comes into play and is so important. Because it is easier to stay committed when you are somewhere that keeps you focused. Around people who want you to succeed. When you are in an environment that stimulates, that motivates you inside when you can't find the motivation yourself.

One of my great personal sport psychologists, Matt, said to me:

> "You don't always have to be motivated,
> but you have to be committed."

When you are on the path to your DREAM there will be hard days. You are doing something you love and are so passionate about, but there will always be days where you just don't feel it so much. As much as you love it, you feel tired. Worn down. Stressed. Overwhelmed by the task at hand. You may be stuck in a moment of adversity and questioning why it is all happening.

You are allowed those days. It is okay to feel that way. As your friend, cheerleader and biggest motivator – let me tell you what I wish I had told myself back then. You can be grateful for your path and still find it hard at times. You can love what you do but not like it some days and you can be following your passion with a fire in your heart and just not want to go for it sometimes. That is okay. I give you permission to feel that way.

Those moments are a sign. A niggle.

> Listen

❯ **Is that a sign that you are working too hard and need to allow yourself a break to rest, recuperate and relax?**

❯ **Is that a sign that you need to adjust your path slightly? Change - not the destination but the way you are going about something?**

❯ **Is that a sign that, MAYBE, you aren't on the right path? Maybe this isn't your dream but someone else's you are fulfilling?**

▸ PERSISTENCE

I don't want to give you false hope and make you think that I just waltzed into Australia and starting elevating easily. It was HARD WORK and it took persistence.

Persistence requires force. Pushing forward despite the resistance of the difficulties you face. Persistence happens when adversity meets continued action.

> ### ADVERSITY + ACTION = PERSISTENCE

Like I said, my friends, difficult times WILL come your way. That is part of the plan in this life. You cannot stay away from it. But in the pursuit of the dream, you must keep going and pushing past all the difficulties to peek through on the other side.

The first few months after I arrived in Perth, I couldn't find a job. I was living off of my student loan in Canada. I didn't have a car. I would train, bike and walk to practice. Some days I would hitch rides and sleep over at my teammates' places to get to training for early morning sessions.

One morning, when I woke up it was raining – a torrential downpour. I was somehow under the false impression that Australia had NO winter. I was wrong. It is nowhere near the magnitude of what it is in Canada, but it still got cold. It still rained. It still had storms.

The storms where tropical. Magical, if you are at home sitting in your comfy bed, but INTENSE. One morning I woke up at around 4:30 am to get ready to do my twenty-minute bike ride to training, when I realized it was torrentially downpouring.

The rain was HEAVY and thick. It was pelting down with gusto. But I had to get to training. I didn't have the money to get a taxi, and this was pre-Uber, therefore cycling was my only option.

I put on my rain jacket, which I had only brought for aesthetic purposes, because I thought Australia didn't have winter. I had left all my winter stuff in Canada. I stuck on my helmet and cycled to training. I might as well say that I swam there, because that is what it looked like by the time I arrived. I was a drowned rat. Soaking wet to the bone, looking like I had jumped in the water fully clothed.

On mornings like that my heart felt a pull for home. A lump formed in my throat and I wished I had someone to call, a person to give me a ride or a family member to borrow a car from. But it was just me. Me and my synchro family who were doing their best too and working hard yet struggling in their own ways.

I had a few jobs throughout my years of training in Perth. But it was difficult to hold down a position when we had to travel so much for training. Financially, it was stressful. My partner at the time, Lexi, was working full time and helping to cover the everyday things like rent and bills. I had to ask my parents to help out for the synchro fees we had to pay to be part of the team. Whatever I earned would cover food and small miscellaneous items. It took a village that was much larger than just me. It was a team effort on so many levels.

There would be days, when I was in Perth, that I would work at the bar until one in the morning, walk fifteen minutes home. Snuggle up in bed for four hours, until I had to wake up at 5am and run to the pool. You see if I ran, it made the thirty-minute walk only fifteen, and I could squeeze in a few more hours of sleep to get me through the four hours in the pool.

There were days when Lexi and I would have to break open our money tin where we kept spare change to pay for bills or food.

There were days I would collect the spare change around the house and the car, add it to what was in my bank account, and walk to the grocery store with $7.50 to make a meal for dinner.

It was hard. Don't get me wrong. There was struggle. But despite ALL of that – I was still passionate, determined, in love and EXCITED about what I was doing.

In the big picture, yes this was all only a few years of my life that led me on an impossible journey to a beautiful dream. But sometimes, when you are in it, it can feel long and hard. Remember, my sunshine-friends – that is okay.

One day, I came home from training to Lexi, who was patiently awaiting my arrival after work. I walked in and just burst into tears. I was exhausted. From the stress of always pinching pennies, from the training day-in and day-out, from CON-STANTLY having to be on my toes at training and improving to stay on the team. I was exhausted from never feeling like I had had enough hours in the day to sleep and exhausted from being homesick. I was so caught up in that moment. I had days, weeks, months – another year and a half at that point until the Olympic Games - if I made it there. I just couldn't fathom HOW I was going to do it and continue to push forward through it all. I sat there sobbing to Lexi who was preciously consoling me as much as he could. I allowed myself to feel it all.

Then I thought about it all. I asked myself those questions. Yes, that was a sign that I probably needed to give myself a little break. Rest a bit more to build up a bit more sleep. Take a bit of pressure off of myself at training.

But despite all of the stress and being overwhelmed, I wasn't dissuaded from my path. There was desire and drive inside of me to succeed. The drive to keep working towards the light at the end of that tunnel was inside me like a raging fire.

I wasn't looking at the steps because, in that moment, I was focused too much on the end goal. The distance between where I was and where I wanted to be seemed to vast. I was looking up for too long. Walking towards my goal without looking down at the steps.

▶ SHORT SIGHTED STEPS WITH A LONG-TERM VISION

In the pursuit of our dreams we need to live short-sighted, and only put on the glasses that give us the clear, distant vision every so often.

I had a moment. I allowed it all out. I released the emotions and moved forward.

Let's play out a little scenario here. Imagine your most prized possession is somewhere on the top of the roof of your house. A two-story house, and you can't reach it by just jumping. As we all know, unless you are some crazy gigantic human being, you aren't going to be able to get the thing off of the top of the roof of the house without some help.

That thing on the roof is your dream.

Most people in that situation wouldn't be silly enough to try to just keep jumping until they are able to reach it. Even if you are an Olympic high jumper you ain't gonna reach the roof through jumping. But that's what SO many people do when they set off on their dreams. They have their eye on the prize and they just keep jumping. They just keep jumping towards their goal and don't understand why they can't reach what they were going after. Confusion, discouragement and disheartenment arise and then they give up. Suddenly the fact that they can't magically jump 10 meters in the air feeds into their limiting self-beliefs that they are not enough, worthy or capable.

Now, let's say this hypothetical person we are speaking of is you, and I am your neighbor. As your neighbor, I am sitting in my house watching you aimlessly jumping like a kangaroo with delusional hope that you are jumping to reach that roof-top dream. As an outsider to the situation, I have a little third-party perspective.

Why don't you use a ladder?

> ### Use a ladder.
> ### Keep your head down, focusing on
> ### each step-in front of you,
> ### With a glance up at the destination just
> ### once in a while.

Then you will get there. One step at a time. I know it may seem simple. But we like to over-complicate things in life.

Now maybe you are one step ahead of me and you already have the ladder with the steps along the way. But you are just so whole-heartedly excited about grabbing that thing on the roof that you try to climb the ladder without looking down at the steps.

What is going to happen? I bet you are going to trip, slip, slide down a few rungs and possibly hurt yourself along the way.

Use the destination as the motivation, but keep your eyes down, not on the prize.

Ten months after getting the golden opportunity, I was walking out on-stage at the FINA World Cup as part of the Australian Synchro Team.

Swimming in both routines, tech and free, I walked out there on stage with my teammates terrified, but empowered. We were so far from the level that we needed to be at! Our team had only been together for a few months and was very young. Our trust in each other and in ourselves to compete on the world stage was a bit wobbly to say the least. But we were so proud.

It was just the beginning. The World Cup was another rung on the ladder. A step to get us to the next level, but we were still so far from the Games.

The following year, we had to go to the FINA World Championships, less than twelve months from our swim at the World Cup, to vie for our spot in the Olympics. Then, IF we qualified, we each individually had to fight for our own spot on the Olympic Team.

In the moment, when we were looking forward – the mountain ahead of us was massive. Our skill level as a whole was nowhere near where it needed to be. We had a lot of work to put in.

The next year our life was a series of countdowns. Countdown to the day off, countdown to our training camp, countdown to competitions, countdown to D-Day – World Championships.

Our team was spread out all over the country in Queensland, Victoria and Western Australia because Synchro Australia doesn't receive enough funding to be able to fund a full-time centralized program. So our life consisted of a few weeks of training in our home cities with our clubs, then jetting off to the AIS (Australian Institute of Sport) for a few weeks' training camp stint where our coach, Lisa, would fly from Canada. For each camp each athlete would have a shell-out a couple thousand dollars to pay for the whole thing.

I was very fortunate that with the help from my partner Lexi, my parents and my scholarship at the Western Australian Institute of Sport we found ways to cover it all. Yes, Lexi and I had personal moments of struggle, where we had to be hyper-aware of our spending so that we could cover all the basics. We didn't ever have the chance to indulge – go out for dinner or to a show, but the beauty was that we found all the free activities in Perth. We made the most of our situation. But it put a massive strain on our relationship. He was beautiful in his relentless support and belief in me and never for a moment made me feel guilty for the situation we were in because it was our journey together. However, we had so many arguments that led back to money, finances and the stress of it all on him. Lexi's love for me outweighed every-thing, but it was detrimental to us both. Our relationship was all about my dream, my goal, my plans, my life – and his purpose got pushed to the side.

I felt so much guilt within me that he didn't have the opportunity to go after what he desired when my dream took up so much space in our lives. It was hard. A difficult circumstance to grow a prosperous relationship. Out of guilt, so many times, I would cry to him, saying that he didn't have to be on this journey with me. I knew the strain he was under and I wanted to give him an out. I wanted him to know he wasn't stuck. But he never budged. The entire time, Lexi loyally stood beside me, being the silent partner in the shadows of success. Allowing me to shine my light as I pursued my dream while he held up everything in the background.

As hard as it can be, being an athlete in the journey of an Olympic dream, sometimes it can be even harder for the silent pillars who are the partners in the background. They are the ones who take the brunt of the stress and the burden of the load. They loyally cheer in the stands with pride and comfort in the moments of darkness. They are on the journey, right beside all the athletes, holding them up and not expecting one ounce of credit, because they are fueled by the love of their significant-other. Although we aren't together anymore, for everything Lexi did for me, I will be forever grateful.

All of us had support in our own form along the way. Our parents, friends, co-workers – anyone who stood beside us and believed in us, all became part of our village.

And when you put yourself in the right environment, in the right village, that supports you – getting to that vision is easier. It takes a village to raise a child and a village to achieve a dream. Anyone out there who has done anything beyond their wildest dreams has been fueled by the power, belief and support of their circle. Even if that support is just well-wishers from afar, and belief in your dream in the background – that adds to the power of the possibility of it all.

The closer we got to World Championships, the more our training ramped-up. Our coach was pushing us to our absolute limits beyond what we believed was possible.

On our training camps, we would start our days with a 6km run, followed by a body weight workout and stretch. We would go through our routine on land in something that us synchro swimmers call 'land drill'. Then we would get ready for our first three-hour session in the pool. After lunch, we would have another land session followed by three more hours in the pool. To finish off the day, we would have meetings after dinner, then tuck into bed for sleep, to repeat it all again the next day.

The sheer magnitude of hours that we had to put in as a team is astronomical compared with most sports, but just the norm for synchronized swimming. Synchro is one of the most technical sports out there and requires a phenomenal amount of focus, finesse and dedication. The routines that you watch being performed at the Olympic Games every four years have involved hundreds and hundreds of hours of training. Those four-minute routines are broken down into sets of eight counts so that all athletes can be synchronized. Within the routine there could be hundreds of sets of eights, and every single number has a dedicated movement that swimmers need to memorize, not to mention different patterns that they need to know, facial expressions they need to practice it all whilst holding their breath half the time. The sheer magnitude of detail that exists in every routine requires that level of work before leading up to competitions.

There would be days when I would wake up and my body would ache. My body would be screaming from the pain of not getting enough sleep to make up for the massive amount of work my body was putting in every day. There were days I would wake up and want to roll back over to sleep, because imagining another 8-10 hours of training ahead just seemed too much. It felt there was never enough food in the world to fuel my four limbs to power through the mountain ahead of me. It took persistence. Commitment. Keeping my head down and taking it one day, one session, one hour at a time to keep pushing forward. It took leaning on my community around me. But despite all of that. Every single moment when I put my head on the pillow at the end of the day I still had that fire burning inside me.

When you are putting in that amount of work every day – you have to love it. You have to have some level of drive inside you that stems from deep-rooted passion. You've got to find the little amounts of joy in the everyday. Something inside you that keeps you going on the days when you feel like you are too tried, sore and exhausted to jump back into the cold pool. Day-in and day-out.

What fueled us, as well, was the competition. The reminder that, as much as we wanted to get to the Olympics, we still had an obstacle in our way that made it not a guarantee. And that obstacle was New Zealand.

What many people don't know about the Olympic Games is that it isn't about the best in the world, but it is about world-wide representation across all sports. I can't speak for every sport, but in Synchro at the Olympics – the eight teams that are there aren't actually the top eight teams in the world. Because the Olympics is the world's largest international multisport com-petition, their aim is to have every continent represented in all sports. So, for synchro, that means that each continent puts forward its best team, then the three additional spots are taken up by the next three top teams. Although we all know that there are seven continents, in the Olympic movement they recognize five. Five continents, five Olympic rings – Oceania, Europe, Asia, Africa & the Americas. For Australia to get into the games in synchro, we had to be the top team in our continent, which came down to a face-off between Australia and New Zealand.

Since Rio, the Synchro Olympic qualification process has changed to include ten countries instead of eight

In the previous Olympic Games NZ hadn't actually put up a team to face off against Australia, but in the lead up to Rio, NZ thought they would give it a shot and fight for the spot.

As intimidating as it was to have that competition, fueled with the uncertainty of whether we were actually going to make it to Rio as a country, it was the greatest blessing because it constantly kept us on our toes. Whenever we had moments of tiredness, exhaustion or lost motivation we would remind ourselves of our neighbors over the 'Pond', training hard to beat us – and we didn't want to let that happen. They were our constant reminder to not let ourselves back down or slack off. They were our consistent inspiration and motivation to keep going.

Let's be honest here my friends. In the pursuit of greatness, on the long path to glory, we can all get disheartened. We are human beings, and we lose sight of the end goals on some days and lack the motivation to keep going. I can almost guarantee you that some days you will completely lose your motivation to keep pushing forward. Those limiting self-beliefs will kick in and feed the fear that manifests in excuses, and you will want to give up.

In those moments, it is so important to consciously SEEK out inspiration. It won't always be inside you. The flame can grow dim. But you need to seek out that source of gasoline to REIGNITE that flame. For us as a team in the lead up to World Championships, that was NZ. For me, on my personal days of weakness, it was something as simple as watching an inspirational video on YouTube. Looking up motivational quotes. Or looking back on pictures of myself when I was younger and reminding that girl then of what this girl NOW is doing with her life. Remembering WHY I am going after what I am going after. WHY I am pursuing this impossible dream.

Give yourself the time to seek out that inspiration. It is OKAY to have those moments of weakness and disheartenment – don't worry. We all have them. As long as you KNOW you are on the right path, DO NOT allow those moments to feed into your LSBs.

CHOOSE to rise up.

CHOOSE to be committed

CHOOSE to seek inspiration.

In the synchro world each year has pinnacle competitions. World Championships, World Cup or the Olympics. It goes through a cycle. However, in the lead up to those major competitions, countries compete at Open Championships around the world to practice competing on the World Stage before they get to that year's benchmark (this process in the synchro world has recently changed). In 2015, our team went to Barcelona to compete at the Spanish Open about a month before we would head to Russia for the World Championships. Not only was this an important competition to display our year's new routine for the first time, but also we would be facing off with our neighbor – New Zealand.

Synchronized swimming isn't a sport where you physically compete against your competitors. We each have our turn in front of the judges in the pool then wait for the others to perform. But the face-off is all a mental game in the lead up. We are like peacocks walking into the pool wanting to show off our biggest and brightest feathers to our competitors to scare them off.

In the warm-up pool, in the lead up to the competition days you could feel the tension in the pool. You could cut it with a knife. We would be practicing beside our biggest competitor, working so hard to show off how good our routine was and intimidate them, meanwhile trying not to let them see that you too are trying to get a good glance at what their routine looks like as well.

No matter how well you practice though, it all comes down to the swims on the day. Who can perform the best in the moment and wow the judges? We were intimidated. We didn't want to let them see it, but they were much better than we expected, and they were fighting hard. They were going for us with no holds barred.

And on the day when we both competed we just barely pulled ahead. We beat the Kiwis, but not by much. For us, the gap was too small. We had worked so hard and sacrificed so much that we wanted to create a large scoring range between us and them. So, with one more month to Worlds, we went to town.

Lisa our coach did not hold back. We tweaked our routine and increased the intensity. She wanted to make sure that we did everything we could to pull ahead at Worlds and qualify in Russia. Lisa had nothing but good intention for us, but in hindsight we were all slowly starting to break. More injuries would pop up, accidents would occur, sleepless nights from stress would leave us tired. The signs. The nudges from the good old Universe were starting to peep through.

A few days before we were about to head to Russia, we were practicing a highlight that we were struggling with over and over again. We had a hard time getting it just right. But practice makes progress, right? So we kept going. On one try we threw Debbie up (the acrobat on our team) and she came barreling down on my face. I had instant panic. Whenever I would get kicked, hit and nudged in the head fear would strike its way through me, giving me a flashback to when I had my concussions.

No way. This was NOT happening to me again, right before we were about to compete at Worlds. I was brought to the side, got out of the pool and put some ice on my face. After taking it all in I realized that I wasn't hit on my head, but rather my eye. Luckily, thank you world, no concussion. But I still had to go to get an X–Ray as the sports doctor was worried that I may have fractured a bone in my face.

I was furious. I had to miss the afternoon training session a few days before we were about to head to World Champs! As much as my body loved the rest, when you are at that level there is always someone ready to replace you. We were on a squad of twelve and I had worked so damn hard to be swimming in the top eight for both routines that would compete at worlds! But sitting out of training that afternoon jeopardized that guarantee for me.

After visiting the clinic, I found out that my face was all good and fracture-free, except for the slowly forming black eye. I was relieved, but still panicked about my spot in the team. I found out later that me sitting out of a training session lead to Lisa deciding to swap me out of a routine and become an alternating reserve. Those few hours out of the pool had jeopardized my chances of being able to swim in both routines at Worlds – and I was devastated. This was adversity training.

With only two days left until we headed to Russia, I found out I now had to fight for my spot to be able to swim in the technical routine at Worlds. Lisa wanted to decide who she preferred in the routine. She kept us on our toes, so we had to grind every training session to prove our worth. It was stressful. I could never switch off. I couldn't have a bad moment in training because I knew that could lead to the tick against me not swimming at the competition. But Lord Almighty, did that create a fire in me?

I had that fear, that scarcity, that worry. But I chose to use those feelings to fuel my fire not deplete my flame. I visualized myself swimming in the eight. I pictured what it would feel like. I thrust all my confidence into believing I could do it and worked my ass off to get there.

Two days before we had to compete our technical team routine Lisa announced that I would be swimming. Relief washed over me the moment she spoke those words. I had proved to myself again that it was possible. With the right tools, what I believe is what I can achieve. My heart felt full. But it wasn't over yet. We still had to beat NZ.

The way it works for international continental qualification to the Olympics is - whichever team has the higher total score – qualifies for the games. So the two totals of the technical and free routines are added together. It didn't matter if they beat us in one, and we beat them in the other – either one of us had to come out on top overall.

I wish I could say to you that we were confident and waltzed in on the day of our first routine and knew we had it in the bag, but we didn't. We were shaking in our boots. There were twenty-five countries swimming their routines, and we had pulled a horrible draw. A few days before the competitions all of the draws are randomly pulled out of a hat. Although technically the draw shouldn't make a difference, it is common knowledge in synchro that you want to go as close to the end as possible. And you definitely want to swim BEFORE your biggest competitor if you have the choice. For both routines, we were pulled at the beginning, before NZ. We felt like the cards were already stacked against us.

Despite the adversity, that was out of our control. As Brian, our sports psych, said – "control the controllables". So we had everything else set in place. We knew our pre-competition plan. We were prepared. We visualized. We were unified as a team. We were as ready as we could ever possibly be.

Competing in Russia was like nothing any of us had ever experienced - or really many people in synchro in general have ever experienced. Because Russia is a dominant force in the world of synchronized swimming the sport is massively popular there. National team athletes are celebrities and they are treated like royalty. So, when the World Championships were coming to Russia, they made sure synchro was the focus. In the city we were in, Kazan, they decided to turn the massive soccer stadium into the synchro pool with 15,000 seats. Thousands more than any synchro swimmer is used to having in the crowd. The roar of the cheering was so powerful that you could feel it reverberating through your body. Focusing on what we had to do for us, amongst the thousands of eyes peering down on us was challenging. But we chose to step up. So on the day of tech. team we went out there and swam our hearts out.

Was it the best swim we had ever done? No.

But it was just barely good enough. We were ahead of NZ by only 0.8 of a point. It was too close for comfort. We knew that if they had a really good swim in the free routine, they could pull ahead. We were still terrified that our collective dream could be snatched from us. But it was theirs as well, right? Only one team could have that dream come true.

It all came down to our free team swims. Our draws were against us. We were swimming second and New Zealand was 22nd. It couldn't have been much more in their favor. But we were not going to let that get us down.

Standing in the last-call room, ready to walk out on stage and perform, we couldn't have been any more nervous. Fifteen thousand people were watching. Our families were in the crowd. Cameras were in our faces and the pressure was on.

The feeling you have when you are about to walk out there and perform at a competition of that magnitude was like nothing I had ever experienced before. Your fight or flight system kicks in and all you want to do is run away and get the hell out of there. My body tried to trick myself, making me think I constantly had to go to the toilet, even though I knew I had let out ever last ounce of pee. My mouth got dry and my body got light. It took everything in my power to bring myself back to the present moment. To not think about all the pressure, all the sacrifice, all the hard work that had led to that moment. What was most comforting amongst it all was knowing I was going out there with my team. My army. My synchro soul sisters who I trusted with my life, knowing that we were in it together. Knowing that I was not standing alone but standing with my tribe, for my country, ready and willing to go out there and give it everything I had inside me.

They announce "Australia".

Our team captain counts – "5, 6, 7, 8."

We walk on.

We strike our pose.

The referee blows the whistle.

The cheers of the crowd die down as I hold my position doing everything in my willpower to not let my limbs shake.

Straight ahead of me I see our team in the Megatron, reflecting back at us.

I look into my eyes and I know I have the power inside me.

The music starts.

Its 'go' time!

When you are doing your routine the feeling is like no other pinnacle of exhaustion that I have ever felt. Your body is on autopilot, knowing each movement so precisely that you could do it in your sleep. As hard as the routine is, it isn't the hardest part. The hardest part is fighting the mental battle. Convincing your lungs that they can survive without oxygen even though they are screaming at you for air. Reminding your legs to fight the excruciating lactic acid that is pulsing through them. To continue to move them so you stay above water. Fighting against the urge for your arms to give up on keeping you upside-down out of the water from pure fatigue. And in the meantime changing patterns with teammates, eggbeater up into highlights to get teammates to fly out of the water and refusing to let it look difficult through that smile on our faces.

It is like nothing else. And the entire routine, four minutes long, goes by in an instant. As fast as it has started, it finishes. Before I knew it we were standing up there on stage receiving our scores. 75.

Not as high as we were hoping, but it was just going to have to be good enough. I took in the moment with pure pride. Knowing that quite possibly that could've been 'it'. That could've been the last time I swam. At least, if we didn't make it, I appreciated it all.

Now all we could do was wait and see if it was good enough.

By the time the competition got around to number 22 it was almost an hour-and-a-half later. We had all showered and washed our hair out, taken off our stage make-up and just had to wait.

We gathered around as a group in the warm-up pool watching NZ on the massive Megatron in front of us. I have never felt so sick from worry in my entire life. I wasn't sure if I was going to pass out or throw up. They walked on, the music started, they dove in and they were doing great! Way better than expected. They were having an amazing swim.

I started shaking my head because I thought it was over. It had to be. They were going to beat us. I started to talk myself out of the dream. The disappointment. I was face-to-face with the fear of "failure" and it was terrifying.

They could get no more that 76, because if they did, then they would close the gap and beat us. As they stood up there on stage waiting for their scores I was squeezing my teammates hands so hard our knuckles were white. But it didn't matter. I wanted to run away. I wanted to hide. I didn't want to know the outcome.

I was shaking my head as tears were welling in my eyes, convincing myself that we didn't do it. Then their score popped up.

73!

From the depths of my soul and the deepest, most vulnerable part of my heart I started wailing. Instantly, hot tears were pouring down my face. My coaches were jumping up and down, my team manager was throwing her arms in the air. My teammates and I were going from hug to hug, squeezing the love out of each other.

A montage of my life flashed before my eyes. The opportunity from Julie. The decision to move to go for it. Leaving my family and moving to Australia. Every early morning training. Every hard training session. All the moments when I doubted myself. Each time I felt my limiting self-belief arise inside me but chose to overcome it with love and belief. Every time that young, insecure and overweight girl was afraid to believe in herself. Every single second of my life that led to this exact moment.

Qualifying the Australian team for the Olympic Games.

Chapter 5

I - IMPROVEMENT

"If we are not growing, we are dying"

– Tony Robbins

Well that is a little bit intense, isn't it, Tony? Way to be dramatic. Calm down!

Okay, well maybe we should think about it for a minute. Give the big guy the benefit of the doubt that maybe he does know what he is talking about. Maybe he ain't that crazy.

Think about a plant. If it isn't growing or blossoming into what it is meant to become – it is dying. Think about ourselves, we go through life – grow up, grow old then phase out and die. I mean it is a little bit dramatic, but it isn't incorrect.

Now, what if we apply that same idea to our mindset, or mental state, or the growth of our soul?

Improving. Growing. Rising into the true self that we are meant to become is part of the whole journey. It is integral to our dreams. And it is the cornerstone that many people miss. They set out, fueled by faith and self-belief, they go after their dream with open arms, they take action, they leap into fear – then they fall. They are hit with failure, are thrown backwards and shoved to the ground by life. However, they get back up and go again and again and again. But the same darn thing keeps happening. They never seem to "succeed", they never find their stride and they never achieve their dream.

Then all the nay-sayers around them use them as the scape goat for why they shouldn't go after their dreams, because Bob-down-the-road tried, and it was too hard. Well, let me tell you something amigas – I bet you Bob down the road was missing a few things through his set back.

CHOOSE to LEARN from EVERY SITUATION

Shock. That's what we felt like the evening after we found out we qualified Australia for the Rio Olympic Games. Initially there was ecstasy and over whelming joy. Tears were flowing from all of us, having literally just seen our dreams manifest in front of our eyes. We hugged our families in the stands, went and celebrated the success and the end of the competition with a bit of champagne, then headed back to our accommodation. That's when the shock hit.

Now what? What was next for us? We were twelve months out from the Olympics and individually each of us still had to make it onto the team. I remember looking around at my teammates that evening as we all were scrolling our phones and updating our loved ones overseas and thinking – this is just the beginning. The battle has only just begun.

A big reason why I did synchronized swimming was because I loved the camaraderie. The friendships. I loved working with other girls who had become some of my closest friends along the way. I loved experiencing life, competitions, struggles, hard times and joyous times with the beautiful women around me. It was better together. I had never really desired to do an individual sport because I LOVED working with others. But I realized the day after we beat New Zealand that everything was going to change. It wasn't about fighting for our country anymore. It was about fighting for ourselves.

There were twelve of us on the squad. We'd had our ups and downs but for the most part we were all as thick as thieves. The best of friends. But three of our friends wouldn't be with us in a year's time. Only nine could make the Olympic team and only eight would swim in the water at a time.

I realized that really, for the first time in my life and my synchro career, I had to stop thinking about everyone else and turn that focus inward. If I wanted to make it onto that Olympic team, every day I had to do what was best for me. Improving myself internally and externally so that I could put myself in the best position to make it onto that team. It wasn't about working harder anymore, because I knew each of us were going to fight tooth and nail for our spot, it was about working SMARTER.

We are living in a world now where, being completely honest, a lot of people work hard. It is the norm to be a hard worker in our day and age because those are the conditions of the society in which we have been raised. We are born and bred to work hard.

That hard work looks different for every single one of us, but the output that we do in the right situation is always the same.

But the people who truly "succeed", the ones who stride forward faster than the pack are the ones who OPTIMIZE their work. They figure out how to work SMARTER.

Now you may be questioning – "That's all well and good, DK – but HOW do I work smarter?"

You're a little beauty – aren't yah? That's exactly what I was hoping you would ask! I have a little equation that will help you get there. It is going to seem overwhelming at first but just bear with me. We will work through it together.

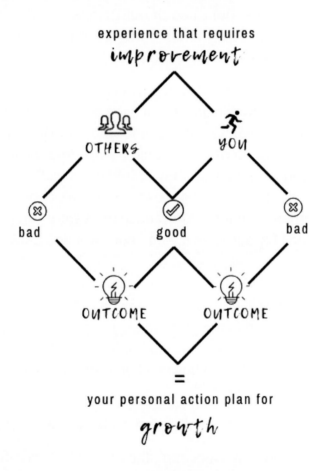

HOWEVER – before we can understand how to work through that bad boy, we must understand that that whole equation can ONLY be optimized when we are looking through the glasses of...

SELF AWARENESS

To be completely honest, self-Awareness is something many people lack. Many people walk around blaming, pointing fingers and attributing their problems to someone else.

- I failed the test because the professor was a bad teacher and I didn't understand the subject.

- My business failed because the economy was on the down turn.

- Everything on my vacation was horrible because the weather was bad.

- My weekend sucked because my kids were sick and my in-laws were visiting.

- I am sick because everyone at work has a cold and they passed it onto me.

- I don't love my physical self enough, because my mum struggled with her body image and passed that onto me.

What if we shifted all of that around? What if we held a mirror up to every single blaming and accusatory comment that we made and see how we brought that into our own life. Into our own existence. That is self-awareness.

- I failed the test because although the professor may not have been the best teacher, I didn't take enough initiative outside of class to seek extra help and learn the material.

- My business failed because I didn't take on the financial advice of my advisor, despite his best efforts to try to help me cut costs, during the financial downturn

❯ My vacation was horrible because I chose to let the weather get me down and didn't make the best of having fun despite the rain.

❯ I am sick because I know I haven't been taking care of myself enough recently, so when everyone else was sick at work it was inevitable that it would be passed onto me as well.

❯ Although my mum did struggle with her body image, I perpetuated that struggle in my own life by taking on her ideas as my own and not choosing to love myself.

Self-awareness is hard. I will give you that. It takes staring at ourselves in the mirror and facing-off with our own demons. Owning our mistakes and taking responsibility for our actions where we have to push our personal dignity and pride to the side and admit that we may have been wrong. Self-awareness is the hard road.

The best way to work on it is using that mirror and facing your...

REFLECTION

The beauty is that you don't always have to hold up your own mirror. You can use the support, love and conversations with the ones around you to allow that reflection into your life. As important as it is to be able to look ourselves in the mirror, sometimes we aren't as good at seeing ourselves. We become so used to living in this body on earth every day that we don't notice our own patterns, habits and behaviors. How often have you had a conversation with a close family or friend where they point out something about yourself that you have never thought of? Never noticed? Sometimes what they say can trigger something inside us. It can come from a place of love in them, but it strikes a chord with our limiting self-belief. The fire inside us flares up and we immediately jump to our defense; but with time, when we sit back, listen and let that comment ruminate in our mind, we realize that maybe...they were right. As much as we may not like it − that is something that we can improve upon.

That flare-up inside us − the one that might struggle with that constructive criticism or personal feedback is our good old not-so-little...

EGO

The ego is the beautifully powerful part of us that likes to go into battle. It is like a feisty little chihuahua inside us that likes to always defend our actions, stand up for ourselves, prove that we are right. The ego is a part of us that makes us human. But the ego can STOP us in our tracks from achieving our dreams if we allow it to run the show. It is something that we need to be aware of − notice its fury and allow the flame to settle. But also know how to step through that fire to our dreams on the other side. Stepping through that flame takes courage. We will need to allow the fear inside us to subside and remind ourselves that on the other side of that flame is massive growth that will give us the next step on the path to take us to where we want to be.

The act of stepping through that flame is the process of self-awareness. Sometimes our friends and family will help us take that leap and sometimes we will be brave enough to do it on our own. But know that GROWTH does not happen without SELF−AWARENESS. How to improve your own self-awareness?

Hard Questions:

1. **From yourself,**

2. **From others.**

At the same time, self-awareness is a fine balance. Think of it like learning to walk a tight rope to maximize our growth through accepting our failings but also learning how to stand firm in our power to build our confidence. However, sometimes if we become too self-aware, then we become self-deprecating. It can lead to a level of self-sabotage where we pull ourselves apart too much, to the point where we lose who we are. We know that we have fallen too far into self-deprecation when our self-reflection opposes our morals. Our questions, steps towards improvement are not aligned with the values that make us who we are. When we are in the depths of self-awareness, looking our true self in the mirror and ready to take action to grow, it is important to ask ourselves:

> Is the ACTION I am about to take in alignment
> with the values of who I am?

Many times in my own life I have stepped too far into self-awareness. I swear I am apologizing for my actions and taking blame in situations where I should have stood my ground.

Cassie, the one with whom I originally started my Olympic dream, taught me so many beautiful lessons in self-awareness vs. self-sabotage, because she challenged me every step of the way once we moved to Australia. Despite what we thought it would be like being to friends going after an impossible dream – it wasn't quite all sunshine and rainbows.

I moved to Perth a few months after Cas, since I had to sort out the logistics of my Aussie citizenship where she already had hers. But our friendship had changed much before that.

We didn't grow up as friends but developed our strong connection at the end our high school synchro career. Having fun, bubbly personalities, our friendship was like a wild fire. We had the best of times together, taking the world by storm. Every hang-out was an epic adventure and it seemed like, when we were together, we saw the world through rose-colored glasses of possibility. Cassie was a blessing in my life. She brought me so much happiness amongst all my other lovely friends. I quickly introduced her to my group of high school friends and we all got along so well. So, when a couple of my high school best friends, Mara and Steph, and I decided to backpack around Europe the summer after our university exchange, Cas jumped at the opportunity to come with us. It was an adventure of a lifetime and I will hold those memories dear forever.

Cassie helped me so much through the pain I felt during my concussion, loyally always being at the other end of the line despite the three-hour time change when I would call her up in heartbroken tears, feeling like I was being swallowed up by darkness.

When she got the golden Olympic opportunity from Julie – she jumped at the idea that the two of us could do it together. Move to Australia, make the team, go after a dream and be best friends and Olympians. We were so excited to have each other on the journey. But that feeling didn't last for long.

As soon as we got back from the first training camp in Perth I felt a change in her. It wasn't about what was best for the two of us anymore, it was about what was best for each of us individually. I started to realize that maybe we weren't as 'together' in it as I thought.

Cas' Aussie family lived in Perth so moving over was a bit easier for her since she had someone to stay with. At first I thought I would be able to get in on that deal as well but, with time, that didn't seem to be the case. I ended up sorting out my own place to live and realized that she maybe wasn't someone I could rely on as much as I had initially thought.

In the pool, during training a similar shift was happening. Cassie would make passive-aggressive comments here and there. Her energy was off whenever we had to work together in drills. She was particularly harsh and critical towards me. The self-awareness in me started to make me think that maybe it was just me, maybe I was making it all up and maybe she didn't feel as cold towards me as I thought. But one day it all blew up.

After training one morning the rain was bucketing down. Perth winter was in full force and the monsoon rains had set in. I would usually walk to the train station to make my way home, but Cassie kindly offered to give me a lift to save me from the rain.

After being in Perth for about two months at this point, I was really starting to get irritated at the way she was treating me. I felt like it was different. So I built up the courage to bring it up to her. And let me tell you – that caused the kettle to blow its lid. That question caused Cassie to let it all out – fast and angry.

Any sort of confrontation with a raised voice makes me immediately uncomfortable. I want to wrap up myself in my shell and hide away. I sat there confused. In shock and in awe that someone who I thought was my best friend had so much anger stored inside, directed towards me. It was pouring rain outside, no one was around to hear us, and I felt trapped in the car. She reached the climax of her fury as she finally spat out – "You are stealing my dream!"

My heart shattered.

I was heartbroken that she could think that of me. She was the one who asked me, told me that I could do it too. She convinced me! And now she was angry that I was doing exactly what she had asked. How could she think I was stealing it from her? Couldn't we be going after it together? That was the plan. A joint dream. It wasn't me versus her. But she thought that it was. It was clear now that she saw it that way.

Because I was never supposed to be an Olympian, I believed that so did she. Therefore, when I got to Australia, came to Perth and started training with the team and was improving – quickly – that was something I don't think that she ever expected. I believe it struck a chord in her. It struck fear in her own limiting self-beliefs that she was struggling with. And instead of working on her own LSB's, improving her own confidence and her own growth – she focused on fear. Fear that I would be better and improve faster – and then that is exactly what happened.

After saying to Cassie with a bruised heart – "Can't it be both of our dreams?" I walked out into the monsoon and let the rain hide my tears. I felt like I'd had my heart ripped out of me. Cas was the only person I felt I had in my corner on this side of the world and clearly she had so much anger towards me. I felt so completely and totally alone. That was only the beginning of our friendship unravelling. I built up a wall in my heart towards her.

I tried over and over again to overcome that wall with love for her. Multiple times we would have arguments where she said I was being a bad friend, I wasn't there for her as much as I used to be, I was cold towards her, I had changed - all of these different things that I took on through my own self-awareness. I empathized with her. Maybe I was doing all those things? I never wanted to be too self-righteous to not take on the reflections of others. I was always aware to hear and digest what others had to say. But the comments kept coming and with each comment a new brick was added to the wall in my heart towards her.

As much as I tried to love through it, each brick in the wall towards Cassie added toxicity in me. I started to feed it. I talked behind her back. I told my other teammates what she said to me. I reveled in gossiping to others about the pain that I felt about our friendship. Yes, it was venting, and maybe I was getting it off my chest to allow myself to move through those emotions – but I know that I went way beyond that. Many times, I could've stopped but I didn't because the toxicity felt good. My heart was hurting so badly from the pain I had allowed her to cause me that I kept trying to make it feel better with all the shit-talking – and, let me tell you, it never did.

At the time I didn't know the power of what I was doing, allowing into my life – but with hindsight I am not proud of all the things I said. I know there were many times that I should've stopped speaking but I didn't because I thought it would make my hurt feel better. I wish I'd had the power to rise above the situation, but I didn't.

I know that Cas said harsh things, I know she was in the wrong many times but so was I. Because...

> ### HURT people HURT people.

Admitting those wrongs wasn't easy at first. My ego wanted to defend my actions and say that she was MORE in the wrong - so I was right. My ego wanted to play the victim and say it was never my fault. My ego wanted to make others feel sorry for me. But self-awareness in admitting my wrongs allows me to grow.

Because dreams do not come without growth. If we are not growing we are dying. That growth doesn't come easily. The hardest times are when we realize – that WE are wrong.

Let me tell you, at the time, in that moment, I didn't have that self-awareness, because I was hurting. But looking back, I know I was no angel in the situation.

When I looked at the VALUES that make up the foundation of who I am – I saw that I was wrong too.

A way to navigate through self-awareness is always bringing ourselves back to our values. The things that make up the building blocks of who we are as a human beings on this planet. What is important to you, beyond EVERYTHING else? What do you always come back to? What is the essence of what makes you tick in this world?

One of mine? Being the best version of myself in this world that I can be, so I can fully love and give to others. That comes from loving myself first, which helps me love those around me. And it also comes from being kind to myself, so I can be kind to those around me.

When I matched that value up with my actions around Cassie – I was out of alignment.

Reflecting on those actions within myself showed me how I was out of alignment with how I was showing up in the world, but on the other side of that coin – who I was surrounding myself WITH so that I was consistently able to show up as the best version of myself in this world.

Remember, my beautiful friends, this universe is kind when we listen. She was giving me little niggles. Nudges along the way, showing me that maybe that friendship wasn't in alignment with my path any longer. I just wasn't ready and didn't have the self-awareness to listen just yet.

So – as she does – the big old and beautiful Universe brought in the big guns to wake me up.

A few months after World Champs we were deep into another training camp at the AIS. About ten months out from the Games and five months out from Olympic Team Trials, our coach, Lisa, was putting us through the wringer, testing our limits. Our days on camp were getting longer, the rests were getting shorter and the workouts were getting harder. It was relentless, and we were all starting to break.

As Brian, our team sport psych, would say, Lisa got "Olympic Fever", where you get so wrapped up in the mission, heading towards the games, that sometimes you forget about the reality of the situation. Her getting wrapped up was the intensity of our training and the reality was that our bodies weren't keeping up. To this day I know that Lisa had no bad intention. She was just doing what she thought was best for us. She wanted us to be great by the time we got to Rio. She just wasn't realistic about the process of doing that.

We would start our days with a 6km run, followed by a hard 30-45-minute land workout. We would land drill (go through our routine on land) before we all rushed to the pool, changing while we were walking, to follow Lisa's strict time schedule. We would jump into a water workout and hypoxic set, followed by drills and music practice for the duration of the three hours. The water training was something that we were all relatively used to, but the intensity she had us at, so far out from the games, was boggling our minds. We had barely finished choreograph-ing our routine, and she took us through four fulls of the routine in a row. To the point where we didn't even know fully what we were doing and still had to swim the full routine. It was truly a safety hazard. And that was just the morning session.

We would have a lunch break, then back to our rooms to lie down for half an hour. We would then go and do an hour of ballet/stretching in the afternoon. That would be followed by another three hours in the water in the evening. A quick dinner then team meetings that would sometimes last an hour and a half to two hours.

By the time we got to bed at night we were all so wound up from the intensity of the day and training that many of us weren't sleeping. We would wake up having synchro night-mares and be counting to eight in our dreams. Our bodies started to run on autopilot. We were doing so much that it literally felt like I couldn't eat enough food at meal time to fuel me. If we got too full, we would feel sick when training in the pool, but within a few hours it felt like my body wanted another meal. Some evenings I remember going to bed with my stomach grumbling from hunger, even though I had eaten a full meal only a few hours earlier – because my system was burning through food so fast to keep me alive. I would wake up some mornings having my body aching from exhaustion, soreness and stress all wound into one. But we would put on our bathers, chuck on our clothes and do it all over again. Counting down the hours until the next rest or meal.

Looking back on some of those days with my teammates afterwards, we realized that we actually blocked it out of our memory. Training at that level, when we weren't prepared for it, caused us to switch off our humanity, detach from our feeling state so that we could make it through. Our bodies were in fight or flight mode. We couldn't run away, so that's how we were fighting.

Despite all of that, I truly am extremely grateful for that time. As difficult as it was, it taught us all how to fight. The power of our mind that exceeds what our body believes it is capable of. And we learned the beauty of binding together as a team to get through that experience together. It bonded us. Because, like I said, Lisa isn't a bad person. Julie who was assisting her as a coach, isn't a bad person. They are beautiful – they cared for us. They were only doing what they thought was best.

But it wasn't sustainable – we knew that, and the board of Synchro Australia knew that.

On the second-last day of our training camp, in October 2015, Lisa came late to our afternoon training session. That never happened. Julie showed up crying. That never happened. We knew something was wrong. During the entire session Lisa was in a daze and Julie was standing beside her with tears rolling down her face – refusing to answer our questions, inquiring what was wrong. We were worried. Although we had hardened to them as coaches, we cared about them as human beings. We were terrified something had happen to either of their families. But we got no answers from them.

Conveniently, that evening we had an athletes-only meeting with Brian, the president of Synchro Australia and also our team sports psychologist. We wanted to express our concerns about the intensity of our training and Lisa's unconventional methods. We knew they were chipping away at us as athletes and human beings. We were being over-trained.

We sat there for forty-five minutes, each getting the opportunity to express our concerns. We let out our problems and released our frustrations. Brian sat there patiently listening and took it all in. Letting us have our moment.

When the dust settled and we all felt like we had let everything out, there was a still, eerie pause from him. We were sitting on the edge of our seats waiting to hear what he was going to do about it. We believed that she couldn't be fired this close to the Olympics, especially with the poor image that would cause for the sport after the issue with the coach after the last games. We were stuck with her – but we just need some changes implemented.

Brian, a middle-aged British man, sitting there listening with his balding head and compassionate eyes, took a deep breath in.

"At 2pm today, Lisa was dismissed."

We all gasped in synchrony. We were in complete shock. Utter disbelief.

Cas, who had received her fifth concussion a few days earlier on camp, ran to the nearest bin and vomited.

What the hell was going to happen now? Ten months out from the Olympic Games and we didn't have a coach.

This was adversity. A massive blow to all of us.

But, like we spoke about before, adversity is PART of the process. Not a byproduct of it. It weaves itself through all of our journeys. It comes in different ways and likes to surprise us to see if we are committed to our dream. It will not stop.

Please remember that although I am sharing with you the process of how I believe you can achieve your dreams through C.L.A.R.I.T.Y, know that it won't always work in that linear manner. The power of clarity is that it is all jumbled up into one big powerful tonic and when you are aware of what you are drinking – you will find your version of success. Because adversity comes countless times, taking action is constant, improving is never-ending and the passion of doing what you love is weaved through it all.

After the news had settled about Lisa, we didn't know if we should laugh or cry, worry or jump with excitement. We were completely and utterly blindsided. We'd had a review of our training and journey to World Champs with a third-party sports psychologist a few months earlier. We found out that, based on the feedback from the reviewer, and other sources, it was recommended that Lisa should be dismissed.

All of us went into those interviews speaking our truth. We had no intention to get her fired. We did struggle with some of her methods, but we also were all really grateful for what she brought us. All of the skills she had taught us and the devotion she invested in us all, to bring us to a standard that helped us beat NZ and qualify for the games.

Now what? Ten months out from the games and we didn't have an Olympic coach. Although Julie was asked to step up to be head coach she decided to resign along with Lisa. Julie also had a young family at home with four children and a daughter under a year old. We knew the stress of traveling with us and staying away from her family was taxing. It was heartbreaking to see her leave as well, knowing she was so close to achieving her professional dream, but the decision was right for her.

So – we flew back to our home states from that camp at the AIS and did all that we could do. "Control the controllables." We had no control over the coaching situation. We didn't know where we were headed in regard to the plan for the team. Everything was up in the air – but all we could do was put our heads down, bums up and train. Train for the next few months until our next training camp at the start of 2016.

In the meantime, I was still on a journey of understanding the tightrope of self-awareness in my friendship with Cassie.

She came back from camp concussed. Having spent the last few days on camp sitting out, resting and wearing sun glasses in the daylight and working on recovering. I cared for her and was concerned for her. This was her fifth or sixth concussion. I was scared for her. As much as I had angst inside myself because of the turmoil ignited between us – I wanted her to be okay. She was told to rest, not drive, not drink, not train and do everything she could to give herself the best chance to heal her brain.

Sitting beside her on the plane on the way home, she joined in with us and had a celebratory post camp cider. I didn't say anything. When she got back to Perth she drove an hour to visit her grandma in a different suburb. I didn't say anything. She went out late with her work friends one evening. I didn't say anything. She asked me to give her a ride to her car the following day as she left it in a different area of Perth overnight – and I couldn't hold it in anymore.

I sent her a text in a group message with myself and Amie as I was walking into a sports psych appointment:

"Cassie, I know you are an intelligent person and know the effects and severity of concussions. I love you and care for you and want you to be in the best position possible to go into Olympic team trials. As your friend I think you should take a look at what you are doing at the moment because I am worried about you."

Maybe I jumped to a conclusions and should've allowed a more generous reason for all of her actions. And in all honesty, I probably should have had that conversation in person and not over text message. The self-awareness in me knows that I could've approached that better. But at the end of the day I know my intention was in the right place. However that lit a fire in her. She was pissed. Angry I had assumed that she had drunk the night before with her friends, approached the delicate situation in a group text message and was angry that I was commenting on her life. I'd had a feeling that would happen, but nevertheless it ripped my heart open once again.

I just felt as if she assumed the worst in me when I know in my heart that I only had the best of intentions. After going back and forth with text messages all day, she called me the following morning.

As soon as I saw her caller ID pop up I felt sick in the pit of my stomach. I am bad at confrontation. It makes me feel sick. As a people pleaser, I like to keep the peace. I don't like people being angry especially with me. I was with Lexi and put the phone on speaker, so I felt like I some emotional support.

Cas was livid. She ranted away on the phone about everything I had done wrong in the situation and had thought the absolute worst in her.

I pulled the phone away from my ear, stopped listening and let her rant. I wanted to vomit.

Then Cassie stated – "I want you to apologize to me for what you did."

Then it hit me. I didn't have one OUNCE of regret for what I had said. It came from a place of love and good intention. A deep care for the long friendship that we'd had. I truly wanted her to be okay. As much as it scared me to write that message – in my core I knew I had to say it because it was aligned with my morals. If I didn't, and something had happened to her, I wouldn't be able to live with myself backing down from my authentic truth because of fear.

Cassie was hurting. I believe her lack of self-awareness and fear of the future led her to project her fears onto me. BUT at the same time, this wasn't the first time. I was ALLOWING this into my life. I had witnessed the signs from the Universe along the way, but until now I chose not to listen.

This wasn't the type of friendship that I wanted in my life. Best friends don't treat each other this way, or at least any best friends that I want in my life. She was striking my limiting self-beliefs left and right – but my ego shone through and allowed me to see – I didn't deserve this.

I am ENOUGH of a friend. I am a GOOD person. I am WORTHY to be treated right. I DESERVE better.

I took a deep breath in and responded – "No."

That is when it all changed for me.

I stood up for myself. Emotionally in that moment and in my heart - I cut the cord from myself to her. That "No" held me, standing in the power of my 'I AM's. That act, as scary as it was, helped add to the building blocks that were becoming my limitLESS self-beliefs.

Self-awareness is a tightrope. It is a hard balancing act of reflection and understanding yourself but also standing in the power of what you believe you deserve. But it is SO important to be aware of our limiting self-beliefs and actively work on improving them because UNTIL we do that we will only attract into our life what we believe we deserve. For a long time I believed that I deserved to be treated the way Cassie treated me. But then I built my own self-worth to a place where I knew I deserved better than that.

To be completely and totally honest with you, my beautiful friends – I had a lot of hurt inside towards Cassie for a long time. I wanted to write this book and expose the unkind things she did to me in order to show the world the victim that I was. Far beyond that exact situation I wanted the world to see her true colors because I was hurting. "Hurt people hurt people."

Through self-awareness, I realized the toxicity that I was holding onto. That toxic emotion of wanting to expose her actions didn't feel good. It wasn't from a good vibration and it wasn't true to my higher self.

However, I realized that I was wrong too. Cas was hurting. She was scared, just like me. She was vulnerable, going after an impossible dream. She was scared she was going to fail, and terrified she wouldn't make it. We both were. We just chose to process it in different ways. She went outward and I went inward. Two girls, similar age, from the same city, same synchro club, moving to the same place, training on the same team, going after the same dream – different outcome.

The difference? I believe it was Self-awareness.

Despite every ounce of pain that happened between us as friends I am unbelievably grateful for every single moment we had together. The good and the bad, the beautiful and the ugly. Cassie is one of the most vibrant, bubbly, excitable, charismatic and magnetic people I have ever met. She was my best friend for a few beautiful years of my life. But I knew, I had to let her go.

Remember –

> our biggest ADVERSITIES
> can be our
> biggest BLESSINGS –
> when we CHOOSE...
> to learn from them.

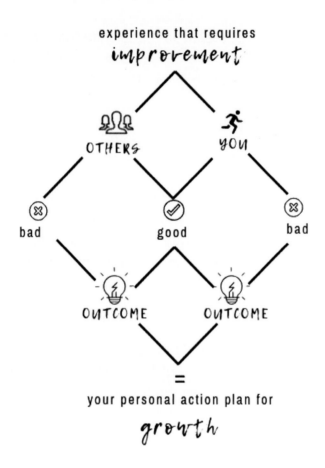

So, my beautiful friends, –

Choose growth;

Choose self-awareness;

Choose improvement; and

Choose love.

Amongst the chaos that was happening between our coaching situation and my dissolving friendship, keep in mind that I was still training for Olympic team trials.

I had come SO damn far from the unconfident, self-conscious teenage girl who had no self-worth and invested all her love into others when I really needed it the most. Trials were only a few months away. So close that I felt like I could taste them. The closeness to "achieving" my dream gave me the laser focus to wind down, go inward and figure out how to make it happen.

Like I said, I knew I could work HARD — but so could all of my teammates. What could I do to set myself apart? What could I do to be different? What could I do to be the exception to the rule that "girls that look like me don't become Olympians"?

WORK SMARTER

Now that we have broken down self-awareness we are ready to approach exactly...

HOW TO WORK SMARTER.

First we need to divide it into TWO categories. Internal and External. You and Others. Myself and Them.

Now apply these questions to your path. Your passion that you are making into your dream.

- **What are YOU good at?**
- **What comes naturally to you?**
- **What do you love?**

❯ **What do you find easy?**

❯ **What are your strengths?**

Self-awareness is SO important when we are asking ourselves these questions because we need to be REALLY honest with ourselves. With our strengths it can sometimes be a bit easier, depending on what level on the scale that your confidence lies. Being an athlete sometimes it was easier to identify these aspects within myself because quite often we would sit down with our coaches and identify them. We would work out and be told what we were good at and what we needed to work on.

If you don't know the answers through your own self-reflection– THAT IS OKAY– phone a friend! Ask for help! Go to your loved ones around you and see what they think. Sometimes, having others hold up the mirror for us allows us to see ourselves more clearly. Sometimes, they can identify things within ourselves that we can't see through our own limited self-awareness.

For me in synchro, my limiting self-beliefs liked to convince me that I didn't have a lot of strengths. Those bloody LSBs wanted to remind me that I sucked and had gotten here by complete fluke and coincidence. But I quieted those mean thoughts inside me and I let my soul shine.

Without getting too synchro-technical on you, these are my...

▸ S T R E N G T H S good

❯ I am strong;

❯ I am tall;

❯ I am a good team player;

- ❯ I have a good work ethic;

- ❯ I have a great attitude at training; and

- ❯ I am good at presentation (smiling & expressing the emotion of the routine which benefits the Artistic Impression mark).

Now, as an athlete, I needed to make sure I was focusing on these aspects everyday so I could give myself permission to shine. I needed to AMPLIFIY the positive parts of myself to set myself apart from my other teammates.

If I was the bloody best at presentation, I was going to be DAMN sure I let that shine through in every repetition. Every time we swam a lap of the routine and every time we did a full of the routine.

Now you may be saying – "Thanks, Sherlock – that is all well and good but there are a few problems. I am NOT an athlete. I DON'T do synchronized swimming. And I am still not quite sure how to apply that to MY life."

I got cha, boo, don't worry. Let's look at it from a different perspective.

One of my BEAUTIFUL best friends, housemate Becky, is currently pursuing her dream of being a highly desired and well-known brand photographer that would give her the personal freedom from financial strain of being tied down to a certain destination with a normal 9-5 job. (She is doing this while I sit here and write this book. We push each other to pursue our dreams together. We motivate each other and support each other - i.e. amigos – ENVIRONMENT is SO important!)

As her friend, I often get the opportunity to hold up the mirror to her life to help constantly improve self-awareness – so in MY opinion her strengths are:

❯ Her stunning photos (@fitfocus_au);

❯ Her photo ideas that lead to great shots;

❯ Her ability to direct clients to hit the right poses;

❯ Her photo editing skills;

❯ Her ability to stay focused on a shoot and get a heap of content in a minimal time; and

❯ Her charismatic, energetic, fun-loving yet friendly and comforting personality that makes clients feel so comfortable during shoots.

She is an AMAZING photographer (book cover shot credit to Becky Felstead). When she focuses on her strengths and allows them to shine through, clients literally flock to her to work with her. Because it isn't just her photos, it's also her personality that makes her truly one of a kind.

Another way to think of those strengths is going back to identifying our G.A.P. Our strengths are our GIFTS. The things that make us 'US'. Becky's gift – she was born with the beauty of her personality. One that is so stunning, when she has the time and space to let is shine through, that people are drawn to her. Another strength of hers is her PASSION. Her ability to take beautiful photos of individuals that capture the essence of people's personalities in her pictures. Her ability to make people fall in love with the images that they see on the screen because years of practice have made her that - darn - good.

Similar to myself. My physique that I was born with gifted me with strength. Strength and power to be able to catapult my teammates out of the water with my pushes that were a little bit better than my teammates. My passion for hard work and a positive attitude at training to constantly improve. These are the aspects that make me ME. That set me apart from everyone else when I give those aspects the chance to shine.

Now what are yours?

Of course we are all human, and have our downfalls. We have the things that we aren't as great at. The things that do NOT come naturally to us. These are our...

▶ WEAKNESSES ⊗ bad

Depending on the level of our ego, self-confidence and limiting self-beliefs, sometimes it can be extremely easy or more difficult to identify these. In regard to the dream that YOU want to go after:

❯ What are the things that don't come naturally to you?

❯ What things do you find difficult?

❯ What are the aspects of the journey that you like to shy away from?

❯ What are the actions/tasks over which you procrastinate the MOST?

❯ What are the things that you just straight-up don't like doing?

If you don't know – remember you can phone a friend. Ask for help. Reach out to someone you love and let them hold up the mirror to yourself.

Identifying these parts of ourselves can be daunting. I know that. It can be scary to be so real with ourselves that we need to identify those things. It's okay. Know that we ALL have those things inside us. NONE of us can be good at everything. It's NOT our job to be good at everything. It is our job to identify what WE are good at and get the others, whose strengths are our weaknesses, to help us with the rest. Let that sink in.

When you are identifying these parts of yourselves, if it hurts or triggers your LSBs – I just want you to know that you are okay. You are enough. You are capable. You are deserving.

And no matter what those weaknesses are – I am still standing here by your side, as your cheerleader.

In the world of synchro I felt like I had SO many weaknesses:

- ❯ my poor posture;
- ❯ my lack of flexibility;
- ❯ my knee-extension;
- ❯ my toe-point;
- ❯ my habit to be off-count of the music when I am stressed;
- ❯ my low body boost height;
- ❯ my poor back flexibility;
- ❯ my habit to bounce to the music.

To work smarter with our weaknesses we have TWO OPTIONS

1. **Work on them**

2. **Outsource them**

Being an athlete, my body's abilities were the key aspect of me "achieving" my dream, so I couldn't quite outsource my weaknesses. That would be nice wouldn't it!?

So I had to work on them. Day-in and Day-out. To work on them the BEST way possible, we need a combination of self-awareness, externally sourcing help from our environment, and persistent action. Identify each point in your weakness and find a plan of action that will help you improve on those weaknesses.

Let's use a different example for yah – back to beautiful ol' Becky.

In the pursuit of her dream, some of her weaknesses:

❱ She doesn't know how to build a website to get her business out there;

❱ She doesn't fully know the best path to effectively follow to help her be a success;

❱ She doesn't know how to write contracts to send to the clients she works with;

❱ She doesn't know the best way to target her social media for clients;

❱ She doesn't know how to design a logo to represent her brand; and

❱ She isn't good with the finances of the business for tax purposes.

Just to name a few. It can be overwhelming, yes – but helpful to actually identify what are the things that are currently holding you back from where you need to be.

With each of those weaknesses Becky has the option to LEARN & IMPROVE or outsource. And that is exactly what she has done.

- ❯ She found website designer to build her site exactly how she wanted it.

- ❯ She got a business coach to help shed light on the best path she should take.

- ❯ Through Google she learned the best way to write contracts for her clients.

- ❯ She asked a friend who is a social media manager how to most effectively get her posts out there online to attract her clients.

- ❯ A graphic designer created her logo.

- ❯ And an accountant she found is helping her with her taxes.

> **Learn and grow,**
>
> **or**
>
> **Outsource.**

When you identify those aspects within yourself, it all becomes so much more manageable. We can break it down into smaller steps of how to take action. Remember the ladder when we were taking about action? Yup. Same thing.

You need to know what you are made of before you can figure out each step. When you start to align that ACTION with IMPROVE-MENT – oh boy, oh boy, amigo – you're gunna start flying.

We know what works for you and what doesn't. We now know where to give it your main energy and where to hold back. We know where to allow yourself to shine and where to allow others to shine for you.

Now – I know what you are thinking. "But DK, that's all well and good – I know my strengths and I know my weaknesses, how do I figure out what the next steps actually ARE?"

You are a little ripper, aren't yah? We are on the same wavelength, I know it. Let me tell you lovely, that's where we are going know. That's where we've got to look...

EXTERNALLY.

So we, human beings, have been on this planet for about 200,000 years. I am going to be completely honest with you friends, I had to Google that. So don't quote me on that – quote Google.

I believe that we are all unique and have our own special passions and dreams to deliver to the world in our own way BUT – we are NOT the first ones to do it.

Even if you are the most individual, trend setting trailblazer in your field – there will ALWAYS be someone out there who has done it before you. It may not be exactly the same. It may be a bit different from you, but there WILL be someone who has gone after something similar before. Whether it be starting a business, being a speaker, writing a book, inventing a product, being a mom, starting a side hustle, making your own homemade soaps – whatever it is – it has been done before.

And this is not to say, 'don't go after it'. Not at all. DO. More than anything, do not be dissuaded by it having been done, because the beauty is – you will do it your own way. You will add the special touch to make it your own magic pudding. And there are people out there who will resonate with YOU in YOUR part of the world, more than they will with the other person. But the beauty of it being done before is that it helps us work...

SMARTER.

Because you can LEARN from what others have done. We don't need to constantly recreate the wheel. We can see how others made their wheel and adjust ours to be the perfect wheel for US! We can see what they did well, that can help us when we apply it to our own life AND more importantly, we can see what they screwed up, what they didn't do the best, what they could improve on. Learn from those mistakes without making them ourselves.

> In the lead up to the Games, our team worked a lot with a sports psychologist. Improvement. As a team we worked with Brian, the president of Synchro Australia and a world-renowned sports psych. You know the British guy that I mentioned beforehand. He worked with us to align our team vision, goals and mission. He taught us how to break down exactly where we wanted to head and how we could do that every day from a performance point of view.

Brian had been to about eight Olympic Games as a sports psych for teams from Australia and Great Britain. He had been beside champions as they won Olympic gold medals and by others who saw their goals disintegrate in front of their eyes during the pressure of the moment. Needless to say, he had experience. He knew what he was talking about and knew what it took for athletes to achieve "success" in their sport.

I distinctly remember him saying, "There has been one common theme in all the athletes who have achieved any sort of success that I have worked with. They all have done this one thing every day. Have a journal, write down their goals and intentions for every day, every training session and keep track of them."

In my brain, "Heck YES!"

That's me. I'm doing it. I'm in. Other athletes who have made it to the Olympic Games have done this one thing that contributes to their overall success in their sport – I would be an idiot NOT to follow suit.

We don't always have to recreate the wheel, my friends.

So that's what I did. I wrote it down.

I broke down my goals for the year, then worked backward. Sometimes, looking at my goals for the year was extremely daunting. As it can be. They were massive. So I took a step back. Figured out my small steps.

I wrote down my goals for the month. Then for the next week. Then for the next day. Going into every training session I would know what I wanted to improve upon. What I needed to focus on to get me to the next level. Exactly what I needed to do each day to improve.

For me, one wasn't enough. I wrote three for each day. Each of those daily goals fed into my weekly goal. Then my weekly goal fed into my monthly goal, which fed into my yearly goal.

I didn't JUST write them down though, I reviewed them every night. I would sit down before I went to bed and be extremely honest with myself:

> Did I achieve this goal today?

> Did my intention for the day flow through my training?

> Did I push myself enough today to make it happen?

In the response to that reflection I would always focus on two things – the good and the bad. What I did well and what I needed to improve upon.

▸ THE GOOD

Allowing ourselves to celebrate and recognize our wins for the day, session or segment of time is SO important. It is our own personal fuel to our burning bonfire of passion. Recognizing our wins isn't egotistical – it is powerful. Because we aren't running around proclaiming to the world how well we did today. We are just sitting in our own personal self-reflection and giving ourselves gratitude for positive action we created.

Even if you had a crappy day – celebrate those little wins. Especially when you had a bad day that is important. It will uplift your mood and lighten your spirit. Even if it isn't aligned with your goals, but just that you got out of bed and allowed yourself to smile.

> Celebrate the small wins.

Then, next we have to step back into our self–awareness and figure out what we can improve upon. We need to be extremely real with ourselves.

> Did we put in enough effort towards out intention today?

We can go to training, go to our job or our passion project and go through the motions. Just tune out and get the job done. Or we can work smarter. Put in the right amount of effort in the right areas to soak up as much from that experience as possible. So we need to be truly honest with ourselves in our reflections. Let me tell you, there is NO point faking it, because the only person that you are hurting is yourself.

Maybe you did put in a solid effort today – YAY! Maybe you didn't and you didn't achieve that goal today – that's okay.

I learned as well, that it was OKAY for me to not achieve that goal within the day. Sometimes the goals that I had for training would be with me every single day until they became habits. I would let those intentions roll over, day-to-day sometimes week-to-week or month-to-month so I could improve upon them. I would set the intention out each day to focus on it, knowing it may be long term but looking at it with short-sighted glasses.

I knew even if I achieved that one intention for the day it wouldn't be a habit just yet. To stick, it needed to become habit.

That method kept me accountable. It helped keep me on track and forced me to be self-aware.

NOW that method – worked for me. BUT this is such an important point to remember through self-awareness in taking on external information.

> ## IT MIGHT NOT WORK FOR YOU!

▸ THE BAD

Honestly, I don't like using the word 'bad', however it is a simple way to describe the polarity of the reflection process. So even though 'bad' has a negative connotation attached to it like our good old friend 'failure', we are going to shift that connotation to –

> ## What we can improve upon.

Don't take everyone's word as law. That method of goal setting and accountability worked for me, but it may not be your thing.

We are existing in a time when it seems like EVERYONE has the answers to everything. Whether it be the perfect diet, the best exercise regime, the only way to raise your children, the flawless five step method to starting a business, the number one way to spend your mornings and the top ranked way to sleep at night. Upside down, in a hammock with your feet wrapped behind your head, hanging from a ceiling like a bat wearing a silk eye-mask. I mean that's how I sleep don't you? ;)

My point is that self-awareness in working smarter is SO utterly important when we are looking externally, because we need to KNOW ourselves and filter out what DOESN'T work for us.

That is the beauty of the time that we are living in. Through a click on the web we have access to every answer under the sun. I believe that majority of people putting that information out there are right. Right for what works for them. But it may not work for everyone. Because we are all different. We all work in different magical ways. That is the beauty of being a human.

We just need to release ourselves of offence and criticism and realize that every human is doing the best that they can in this moment.

I even know that this book, my method of achieving one's dreams, manifesting our magic life – may not be the perfect solution for everyone. That is okay for me. Because I know it will be the perfect solution for the right people. And that is enough for me.

You may be thinking – "Well great DK, how do I know what will work for me and what won't?"

TRIAL & ERROR + SELF AWARENESS

Test it out. Figure out what FEELS best to you. Truly feels best in your gut. Use your self-awareness to decipher the truth. The beautiful part is that the more and more you use your self-awareness the better you will get at it. That self-awareness will become your inner guidance, truth and divine intuition. The more you work the muscle, the stronger it will get. Then you will need to spend less time on trial and error and allow yourself to live more with your intuition.

Something that I constantly need to improve upon in synchro is my flexibility. I would say I am probably more flexible than the average person, but it does NOT come naturally to me. If you saw my Dad in a yoga class, you would understand, genetically, how much of a bloody miracle it is that I am able to do the splits. Bless his big heart, my Dad is a beautiful man, but he can't touch his toes to save his life. He can't even sit on the ground with his legs straight. I did a few hot yoga classes with him, it was a comical experience to say the least. Needless to say, he blessed me with height and strength, NOT flexibility.

I always struggled with my flexibility. My strong muscles don't like to be stretched out; I literally feel like they resist! The more flexible you are in synchro the more ability you have to move your body in different ways. The more movement, the more different positions you can get into and the more creative your routine can be.

So, for years and years, my coaches would tell me to stretch every day. Stretch at home, stretch while watching TV. Do the splits daily. Over-splits as often as you can. Over-splits is where you put your front leg up so that it is elevated, and the goal is to have your legs at an angle that is GREATER than 180 degrees.

Yah. "Ouch!", right?

So I tried. I worked on stretching daily to get my limbs lubricated and moving, but I just kept finding it didn't work. I heard over and over again that that is how you get more flexible and I was so confused because I felt like I was getting worse. And I was! Sometimes my limbs would be so sore from excessive stretching that the following few days my splits would be worse than when I started.

Keep in mind that I have been in the sport for as long as a teenager has been alive — so I had a lot of time for trial and error. I finally realized that that didn't work for me.

I started to notice that when I would allow my body time to recover and not try to stretch myself like a rubber band, I would improve. I would still need to keep consistent, but excessively stretching everyday didn't work for me!

That self-awareness helped me grow immensely. I was told it was the only way to improve. I was told I had to do it because that is what everyone else did. I tried and tried and tried, but finally realized that it didn't work for ME. That was powerful.

Now that's all well and good to describe it in a synchro sense, but let's bring it back to Becky to get another perspective.

When she started working on her personal photography business, she looked externally to see what others were doing, what worked for other photographers doing branding photos.

She saw other photographers taking whatever jobs came to them, because if the money paid well then there was a job to be done. But she slowly started to realize, through trial and error and self-awareness, what worked for her and what didn't.

Becky didn't resonate with taking pictures for larger corporations. She didn't feel like working with customers who had bad energy and she didn't love shooting for photo journalism or the paper anymore. She had no desire to work with clients ONLY for the money. That didn't feel good for her.

So Becky decided to work smarter.

She only works with people who help other people

Whether it be small business selling a beautiful local product or a personal trainer helping individuals get back into moving their body. Whether it be life coaches helping women find their path in life or Olympians writing books and trying to inspire other to go after their dreams. That feels good to her.

You know what the CRAZIEST part of all is?! Ever since she stopped doing only what others said would work and started refining what works for her – business and the right clients have just flowed her way. She is CLEAR about her vision and she is in alignment with herself from her inner guidance and self-awareness.

THAT is working SMARTER.

Now. Time to create our OWN special sauce.

When you figure out your...

STRENGTHS + WEAKNESSES

Make a plan.

Then add in...

WHAT WORKS FOR OTHER vs. WHAT WORKS FOR YOU.

You will realize that you have your OWN personal special individualized plan that helps YOU improve.

When you improve, you grow. When you grow, you move forward. When you move forward, you step more into alignment with your dreams. That is where it starts to get REALLY exciting, my beautiful friends. Because then you start to create MOMENTUM!

Despite all the adversity, heart-ache and confusion that I felt around my relationship with Cassie, the lack of an Olympic coach and the constant financial struggle – I had my plan to work smarter. That method and that consistency helped me every day. It kept me focused and it allowed me to continuously improve along the way.

Things slowly started to fall into place along the way. My friendship with Cas grew naturally more distant, despite training together every day. Synchro Australia found a beautiful young, charismatic and dedicated French-Canadian name Lilianne, who was assigned to be our Olympic coach. She left her life in Canada and moved to Perth to fully dedicate herself to the journey. Lilianne was a tiny and curvaceous thirty-three-year-old with her jet-black hair constantly swept up in a messy bun and always walked around with a spring in her step. She was extremely confident and well-spoken yet her French accent often led her to mispronounce a few words. She was enthusiastic yet disciplined, she was loving, yet pushed us. She saw us all as human beings, not just athletes. We knew that she cared about our well-being in and out of the pool. She was a beacon of light for us in a time that was exhilarating, yet terrifying.

Lilianne moved to Australia in January 2016, eight months before the Olympics. It was another one of those bizarre situations where you meet someone for the first time knowing that you will have an epic journey together, yet at that time they are a complete stranger to you. Slowly but surely, we learned to trust her and to love her. Let me tell you we didn't love her every day, but I don't think you ever should with your coach. You need to get them to push you when you don't want to be pushed. Force you to do the hard yards, especially when you don't want to. In many moments you aren't supposed to love them, but at the end of the day we fully respected her and trusted her. We knew she had what it would take to bring us to the Olympics.

Lilianne came into our lives three months before our Olympic team trials. That was the big event we were working towards. No plans could be made until each of us knew if we were on or off the team. It was stressful. We could feel the pressure between each of us.

Honing in and focusing on myself through my constant striving for improvement, growth mindset and ability to work smarter helped me get where I needed to be. Between our training camps with the National team at the Australian Institute of Sport and training with our own coach in Perth we were preparing for the biggest trial of our life.

Not only was the pressure on because it was the OLYMPIC trials, but also the magnitude of what we had to do for the trials was intimidating.

Four international judges and a referee were flying in from around the world to select the team. From Austria, Great Britain, Japan, Switzerland and Malaysia. Our trial process was over two days, with the third day for the Olympic duet.

One day was for tech team, one day was for free team. For both routines we had to swim them once in front of the judges individually, without the team, to receive a score. Because synchro is a team sport we also had to be individually judged on our swims while swimming with the team. Two athletes would be judged at once during the team swims wearing different colored caps and tape around our wrists and ankles to distinguish us. For 12 athletes to get their time to shine, judging two at once within a routine the team had to swim the routine six times. This meant that within each day we had to swim our routine seven times.

Now, to a non-synchro swimmer that may not sound like much. But that is intense. Swimming a full synchro routine once is like sprinting at full capacity for 4 minutes, while holding your breath for 50% of the time, while having to move all your limbs to the right tempo and constantly change formations with your team. At the end of the routine that lactic acid hits you so intensely it is the worst physical pain I have endured. Swimming to the side of the pool to pull yourself out can feel so difficult that you think your legs might fall off. At training in the lead-up to competitions we may swim through the routine four times maximum. So having to swim seven, in one day was pretty daunting. Not to mention that the six swims within the team were in twenty-minute intervals.

In the lead-up to trials our coach in Perth, Briana, prepared us the best way she knew how. Briana was a 26-year-old American expat who moved to Perth to coach synchro. She studied sports management at university and moved to Perth to pursue her dream of becoming a high-level synchro coach. We were her guinea pigs. She was young, only a couple years older than me, but she was dedicated to us. She put together a detailed plan in the lead-up to trails that we followed to a tee whenever we were in Perth. Briana stayed on top of our training, recovery, injuries and work schedule to optimize our performance. We would train 8am – 1pm every day, followed by recovery in the ice bath and compression boots, go to any appointments with the physio, doctor, sports psych or massage we had after that, then spend the evenings working. We did that, six days a week with Sundays off. About thirty hours a week of training while in Perth, then doubled whenever we went on training camp.

A couple of weeks before our trials, Briana broke us all up during our training and we each had a private session with her. We had time to just focus on ourselves. In preparation for the six swims in a row that we had to do at trials, she was making us do it individually at training to prepare.

I was pooping myself. Well, theoretically not literally. I remember the first day, when I knew I had to do six fulls, I was so nervous. I knew exactly what I needed to do and felt confident in my knowledge, but I was just so scared because I knew how hard it was going to be. I knew the pain that my body was going to feel, and it scared me. But I knew it was only going to help me improve – I had to do it to be prepared and make myself better. I know however, without a coach it wouldn't have happened.

▶ A COACH

Now this is so important, amigos. It is a point that I want to be clear about. A reason why athletes achieve "success" is because of their coaches.

Someone to motivate you, guide you and push you to do the things that you don't want to do. I believe that, deep down, we all inherently WANT to work hard, but actually DOING it can be difficult.

I sit here today as an Olympian who has been in my sport for over 18 years but being COMPLETELY honest with you – no matter what I do, I will always work harder if someone is standing over me, watching and telling me what to do.

Nowadays, there are life coaches, relationship coaches, business coaches, sports coaches and everything of the like – but you don't NEED to actually HIRE a coach to achieve your dreams. It will definitely help accelerate your growth and push you towards where you want to be much faster, especially when you find the right coach who fits you. But, in the most basic sense of the word, it is someone who holds you...

ACCOUNTABLE for your GOALS.

That coach can be a friend in your life, a partner, a parent, a mentor. They are someone who is invested in your growth and will make you take action and stick to your plan. They hold up that mirror in your life to aid you in self-reflection. They will push you when you don't want to be pushed and ensure you are sticking to your word. They will speak the truth. Sometimes that truth may make you frustrated with yourself or may make you want to just walk away all together. But they won't let you. You know why?

Because your coach...

Sees the potential in you.

You want to know something else? I see the potential in you too. I may not know you personally, I may not ever meet you (although I hope I do), but I know the power that is inside you too.

Because, if you are here, reading this book or listening to my voice, there is something inside you that is aching to grow. I know you desire to achieve and become more than you are now and to improve upon the beauty that is already inside you.

I do not know you, but I know who you can be. And I am cheering you on every single, frigging step of the way, I hope that you know that. That's why I am your...

Cheerleader.

Because, along with our coach, we all need cheerleaders in our life, and we can have more than one. But our cheerleader is someone who devoutly believes in us. They pick us up when we are down to remind us of our beauty when we refuse to see it. They show us the power of our shine when we feel dim. Cheerleaders stamp on our Limiting self-beliefs to reveal the power that is inside us. We should all have a cheerleader in our lives. It can be our mom or dad, or best friend or sibling, or cousin or teacher, maybe even just our neighbor next door who sees our shine. I know I am one of them, but you all have more. Even if it is hard to see sometimes, we all have cheerleaders in our lives. Don't forget about them when you are down. And most of all – don't forget to reciprocate. Be the cheerleader in someone else's life too. The more we support each other the more we all rise together.

And in the moments when our cheerleader isn't around, we need to learn how to become our own cheerleader. Learn how to quieten those nasty, limiting self-beliefs, tune into what we truly want, and know who we whole heartedly are and believe in ourselves.

That same day when I had to swim six fulls in a row for the first time, I also learned how to become my own cheerleader.

Walking to the top of the pool where I was about to dive in for my first full, my legs were shaking. I had my head down trying to wrap my mind around what was to come. I felt like I wanted to poop myself and vomit at the same time. My mouth felt dry, even though I knew I was completely hydrated. All the feelings that flushed over me when I was about to compete were swimming through me. Then all of a sudden, as if I was connected to some inner guidance, three short sentences popped into my head. Three sentences that eliminated my self-doubt and terminated my limiting self-beliefs.

> I am STRONG.
> I am CAPABLE.
> I am CONFIDENT.

They became my limitLESS self-beliefs. My affirmations. In my darkest hours and most scared of times, those were the words that I would repeat to myself. Those words pumped through me as I swam my routines six times like fuel in my veins that empowered me to push through.

So, although I was terrified of the possibilities heading into Olympic team trials, I would remind myself of those affirmations every day. In the moments I wanted to run away out of fear when the possibility of "failure" overwhelmed me. Those words made me believe.

One week before the D–Day of trials I was sitting in my room one evening, unable to sleep from nerves. My partner at the time was lying beside me sleeping soundly like a baby, not knowing the hurricane of emotions pumping through me.

I literally felt ill. The amount of nerves I had, moving into the trials the following week, completely overwhelmed me. I was training and recovering and resting and prepping as best I could, but I constantly felt sick. I kept getting headaches from stress and any moment when I would sit in silence, I felt like I wanted to vomit.

The pressure was real. Although they didn't mean to, I felt the pressure that everyone in my village unconsciously placed on me. Being only five months away from the games my family were starting to book flights to Rio, looking for accommodation and buying tickets to events. They were planning all these things, but I still hadn't made the team.

"You'll be fine, don't worry, you will make it!" they would say to me. It was beautiful how much they believed in me now, but it made me angry! All they had to do was sit on the other side of the phone and support me. Cheer me on. They just had to believe in me and buy tickets. I had to do the hard yards to prove myself. I had to do the work and endure the pain. I know it wasn't rational for me to be annoyed with them, but I was in a hurricane of emotions.

Because, although I had my affirmations, my limiting self-beliefs were about to have a face-off with my dreams.

As much as I said "I would rather try and fail than always wonder 'what if"?" I felt like I was about to stare failure in the face. I had come so damn far. I wasn't the unconfident, overweight, self-hating young girl I used to be. I had transformed myself into this athlete that I never would've believed I could be. I had sacrificed so much time with my family and friends. I had given up the chance to be there for the milestones in my loved ones' lives. I surrendered the ability to be financially stable, by relying on my parents and partner to get me to this point. I had dropped out of university. I had moved across the flipping world on my own. And what... what if it was all for nothing?

What if I didn't make the Olympic team?

That was terrifying.

As I was sitting there in the darkness of the night listening to the sound of Lexi's sleeping breath, feeling like I was being swallowed up by the possibility of "failure" – it hit me.

A realization that hit me, so strong and hard that it brought tears to my eyes. It lifted the load from my heart and allowed my soul to breathe. It was like, all of a sudden, I could see with complete clarity.

That moment was the pinnacle in my improvement and, I believe, the reason why I am here today writing this book.

But,

I am going to make you wait. I know, I am sorry! I don't mean to be a tease! I promise you I will share with you what that is when the time is right. Just not yet. When you get to Y – you will see.

I know you probably want to punch me for leaving you on the edge, but just have patience. I've got another little powerhouse of a story for you first.

Olympic Team Trials – April 4 – 5th, 2016

D-Day. The first day. Tech team.

It was one of those days that, in my mind, felt like a movie montage. A montage mashed up with the "Eye of the Tiger" music. Picture me and Rocky putting on our training gear. Plugging in our head phones and getting to the pool. Rocking up and doing our warm-up while the international judges get ready for the day of selections. Me versus all my teammates and best friends. Me against the many. David versus Goliath. Okay, maybe Rocky wasn't there...but in my mind that's what it felt like.

Like everything in my life had brought me to this moment. To these two days where I had to prove myself. Prove my worth. See if I had put in the work to become an Olympian. If I was good enough.

We were warming up in the outdoor pool outside of the Western Australian Institute of Sport in Perth. The girls from WA were really lucky that the trials were in our home pool. We were familiar with the surroundings.

At the start of the day the referee from Great Britain ran us through the day. Tech team elements, individual tech swims. Lunch break. Then the six team swims in a row.

The morning went okay for me. I was pretty happy with my individual elements in front of the judges. My individual swim was solid. There were aspects that I knew I could've done better but overall I was happy with it. It was enough.

In the afternoon though, I could never have guessed what was about to happen.

We were on our second team swim out of six. It was Cassie's time to shine as she was being judged. She put on the pink cap to identify her as the judged one, along with our other teammate wearing a blue one. She strapped her wrists and ankles with pink tape as well. It was my turn to swim after her on the third round. All I had to do for this swim was get through the routine and blend in. The ones who weren't being judged were really just place-holders for the others. It was a bizarre place to be in where you had to swim well enough to blend in with the team and not poorly stand out, but also not exert too much energy so you were prepared for your own judging round.

We walked out on deck, the music started, and we were on. We dove in and it felt like a pretty average swim. It wasn't my time to shine so I wasn't too stressed. We were about two thirds of the way done the routine going into our rocket split element.

Rocket split is a movement in synchro where from upside down underwater you shoot yourself out of the water vertically. You hit your height ideally at about belly button or higher, snap your legs into a 180-degree split position, then snap back to the vertical line while you sink underwater and tuck out back to the surface.

As I was snapping my legs down into the upside-down split position, I felt a SMACK on my back leg.

Cassie and I had collided. We were in line in the pattern and in the split second that were go into the upside-down split position my back leg and her front leg accidentally slammed against each other. I found out later that instead of going back to the vertical line, the collision shocked Cas and she tucked from a split position. In normal circumstances not completing the element correctly would result in a penalty.

I immediately felt sick with worry. I continued the routine until the end but knew in my gut that this wasn't good. I felt horrible.

The routine finished, we all sat up and as soon as we had a moment to breathe I heard a deep painful and soulful cry escape Cas' lips. She was in front of me. I have never, personally, heard any pain so raw and poignant. The sound crept under my skin and struck shivers to my heart. Before she even had the chance to turn around, any oxygen left in me I uttered – "I am SO sorry Cas! I didn't mean to! It was an accident!"

She slowly turned around and gave me a look I will never forget. There were daggers in her eyes and hatred in her heart. If looks could kill I would have been slaughtered. I could feel the pure detestation vibrating from her eyes. She was livid. I wanted to throw up. As quickly as I could I swam to the referee.

In my whirlwind of emotions, I couldn't help but think. "Of course, this happened to me and her. Of course!" It couldn't have been any other two people on the team but the ones who were best friends, moved here together and had a falling out.

It couldn't have been anyone else but me, who she blamed for so many things, that she had collided with.

Maybe it was the Universe's divine intervention.

Ironically, in the lead up to trials when we were asking all different questions about the process, Cas asked, "What would happen if there was any sabotage during trials?"

We were all a little bit shocked as we all hoped that would never happen. However, it wasn't just me, the entire team was having issues with Cas' difficult behavior and inability to work in a team. Possibly it was her subconscious fear that she was bringing to the surface. That thought made me sprint to the referee.

I quickly got out and being still completely puffed from the routine and having tears well up in my eyes from the pain and shock of the situation I blurted out – "I didn't mean to. We collided. It was an accident. I am so sorry! I didn't mean to!"

The beautiful grey-haired British judge said calmly to me – "I know. It's okay. Don't worry. I know it didn't happen on purpose."

Giving myself a moment to think about it though – it wasn't actually my fault. It wasn't Cassie's either. It was completely and utterly an accident. The fact is that the rocket split element literally happens in about two seconds. It is so quick and performed upside down with our legs that you actually couldn't plan it if you tried. I was facing away from Cas and completely blind, in the sense that I couldn't see her behind me. Also, it wasn't the first time that someone had hit someone during a rocket split. It happened occasionally to all of us. Because of the pattern, being stacked in front of each other, it was likely to happen if we weren't perfectly in line. AND when it happened in the past, to other teammates, they all still completed the element and didn't tuck out of it.

Cassie got shocked. She freaked out and she tucked. I didn't make her do that. As well, I was hit too. I continued to swim as if nothing had happened.

All these thoughts were buzzing through my head as I jumped back in the pool to do a quick cool down before it was my turn. I was completely shaken up. I wanted to cry and run away. But I couldn't.

It was an ultimate moment of switching into athlete mode. Turning off the external factors and existing purely in the moment. I couldn't control what had just happened. It was in the past. I couldn't let THAT affect my swim, which was in less than fifteen minutes. I had to shake it off and get my head in the game.

As best I could, I let it go. Brought myself back to the present. It was my moment to shine now. After everything Cassie had accused me of, after every argument that we had. After every interaction where I allowed her to be unkind to me and was unkind back – I wasn't going to let that accumulation affect my Olympic Team Swim.

I put on the pink cap. Taped my wrists and ankles. And it was game time.

In my swim I was convinced that Cassie was going to try and come after me. She was seething with anger and I felt like she was going to try and do to me what she thought I did to her. I was paranoid. I swam the routine on high alert doing my best to avoid getting anywhere near her in our close pattern while still performing the best I could. Was she actually trying to sabotage my performance? Honestly I don't think I will ever know. I like to believe that she was better than that. She rose above it for our friendship's history. But to be honest, I just don't know. So I prepared myself.

I finished and believe that I did the best I could in that situation. Was it my best swim ever? Definitely not. Was I proud of my performance despite the massive curveball that was thrown my way? Definitely.

That evening I was so shaken up. I was trying to process everything that had happened. It seemed like everything we had gone through in our friendship had hit a climax. It felt like a movie moment.

But I had another day of trials. One more day where I had to put my head down and focus on me. I knew the swims on tech day weren't my best because I was so shaken up, so I had to make up for it. There was NO way in hell I was going to allow that situation be an EXCUSE for not performing to my potential.

So that's what I did. On the day of free team, I went out there and let myself shine. Swimming my individual free swim in front of the judges felt like the best swim of my life. I felt unstoppable. I let my strength SHINE. I was high, I presented, I had posture. I got out of the pool at the ended exhausted yet beaming. That was what I knew I had in me all along. If nothing else, I was DAMN proud of that.

Now all I had to do was wait to find out the result.

www.DKbonuses.com

Chapter 6

T – THANKFULNESS

"There are only two ways to live your life.
One is as though nothing is a miracle. The other is
as though everything is a miracle."

– Albert Einstein

We are at my favorite part!

I believe that thankfulness is the combination of...

GRATITUDE + PRESENCE

If you take NOTHING else from this book, I hope you at least take away the power of gratitude and presence in life. Yes, of course, this is part of a step towards achieving your dreams, but more importantly it is a mantra to live your LIFE by!

It is so easy for us to get caught up in the regularity of life through the day-in and the day-out. The normality that is waking up, going about our day, eating, pooping and going to sleep – that we forget how this life is absolutely...

magical

Okay, think about it. We are in these bodies made up of millions upon millions of teensy tiny atoms of hydrogen, carbon, nitrogen and oxygen, that form skin and organs and lungs and eyes and hair and blood and veins. These bodies that we exist in have a heart, which pumps blood through our bodies 24/7. Our lungs autonomously breath in oxygen (which fuels our blood) and out carbon dioxide. Our eyes blink without us consciously telling them. Our legs take steps every day to allow us to walk and run through this life. Our hands give us the ability to reach out to the ones we love. Touch them on their cheek and wipe away their tears. Our lips allow us to speak and communicate words of love with one another, all in different languages that we, as humans, have CREATED throughout history. The receptors on our skin give us the ability to feel love when we are hugged by another. Our two ears are the perfect funnels to hear the waves crash on the shore, the laughter of our friends and the music we love. And if all of those parts of the human body work for you – YOU and I are among the lucky ones – because there are many people who don't have those luxuries.

Why is it that, quite often, it's only when we lose our sight that we appreciate vision? Only when we have our speech taken away from us we see the power of our voice? When our hearing doesn't work that we appreciate the beauty of sound? And when we lose the freedom to walk by ourselves that we realize the wonder that is running?

That is only our body. Don't even get me started on the beauty of this big beautiful round rock that we all exist on that floats in universe while rotating around the sun that sheds light on this planet. And the moon that comes out every evening and has the power to control the tides of the vast ocean.

Magic isn't an illusion. It is real when we allow ourselves to adjust our perspective.

> ## Life is freaking MAGIC!

Sometimes, when we think of gratitude, I think that we all have the tendency to go big, but what if we stay small.

Our family. Our friends. Our house. Our car. Our stuff. Our experiences. That is all beautiful, don't get me wrong, but there are many people out there who don't have those things. What if we focus on the small things? The things that we take for granted, that we can't always hold or touch or sometimes even see.

Think about that:

❯ **What are you grateful for?**

❯ **What are you grateful for that isn't your family, friends, house, car, clothes, or experiences?**

❯ **What are you grateful for that you can't see but can only feel?**

Now that is powerful, hey?

Sometimes we only realize what we are grateful for when we lose it. Let's change that. I am over that mentality in this world. Why don't we appreciate everything WHILE we have it? In the moment. Before it is gone. Because life is always evolving, and change is inevitable. So grasp the bloody beautiful moment right here, right now, as you are.

I challenge you to stop. Right after you finish this paragraph and I say "NOW", close the book. Pause the audio. Close your eyes, if you can. Take a deep breath in and feel. Feel the breath enter your body and fuel your lungs. Feel the air on your skin. Feel the beauty of this moment in complete stillness. Forget the past and let go of the future. And feel how grateful you are – to be alive…

Right…

"NOW."

Beautiful, isn't it?

Although my journey wasn't "normal", I mean what even is normal? I am grateful that it happened EXACTLY the way it did because it gave me perspective.

I didn't ever think that I would get to such a high level in synchro. Never in a million years did I think I would move to Australia and be on the national team. Trying out of the Olympic Team seemed ludicrous and actually being an Olympian felt impossible.

SO, the more and more I proved my limiting self-beliefs wrong and smashed through the preconceived notions of what I thought life could be, the more and more thankful I was.

Every moment I felt like I was living the impossible, and I wasn't going to let myself forget how lucky I was. Of course, some moments were harder than others and I would get caught up in the chaos of it all. But as often as I could, I came back to the gratitude I felt to be doing something that I loved. No matter the outcome. I believe that gratitude all came to fruition on

April 7th, 2016

I had barely slept. It was one of those evenings when the knot in my stomach kept me tossing and turning all night long.

The evening before, my teammates and I all stayed up in our rooms chatting about all the possible outcomes for trials. There was a weird sense of knowing that, in a few hours, our whole entire lives would be changed. We were sitting on the edge of an abyss. Just over the edge there was an incredible amount of fear and faith. Fear of outcome but faith that we would all be okay.

That previous evening we all went out for dinner one last time as a team of twelve. We sat around the table and all spoke about what our plan would be if we didn't make the team. Where we would go, what we would do and how we would cope with it all. It was a harsh reality we had to stare in the face. In the process of going after your dream, especially an Olympic dream, it seems almost counter-intuitive to plan for the possibility of "failure." But you need to have a pinch of realism. It's balancing the relentless optimism while giving yourself a brief glimpse of your backup plan. I didn't have a structured idea of what I would really do if I didn't make the team. I knew it would crush me, but I also had this deep knowing that I would be okay. I would get a job, maybe go back to school, maybe travel. I would pick up the pieces. But I knew most of all that I would be okay.

When we came around to Cassie's turn, her answered shock us all. Every single one of us had an idea of what would be next. Even Bianca, our team captain, 2012 Olympian and shoe-in for the team, but Cas' answer. "I don't need a backup plan because I know I will make the team."

There was an awkward silence that filled the table after her response.

There is the conscious, yet unspoken, knowing on teams about the ranking of each athlete within the squad which becomes an invisible hierarchy between us all. We all had a general idea of who was at the top and who was close to the bottom. From the previous competitions and consistent rotations of the eight that would swim we all knew who was more likely than others to make the team. Rose, a Kiwi import, was by far the best technical athlete on our team. She was naturally gifted at synchro and movements came with ease to her. But even Rose had a backup plan. Cassie wasn't in the top half of the team. She hadn't swum in both routines the previous year and her technical ability was lacking in a few areas. We all knew it was a gamble if she was going to make the cut. But I truly don't think that she knew that.

Self-awareness my friends.

On the morning of the 7th, though, Cas was far from my mind. I was focused on myself.

It was one of those mornings I woke up feeling nauseous from my insomnia the night before. The combination of my body's exhaustion from trials, along with the lack of sleep, swirled in with the nerves, made me feel like I was almost having an out-of-body experience.

Lexi had taken the day off work to be with me to hear the phone call. He picked me up from the hotel that we had been staying in Perth for the trials process and we went back to our tiny little studio apartment.

At 9am Brian was going to start calling us one by one to tell us the result. If we made the team or if we didn't. He would call the bottom three girls who didn't make the team first, then follow through to the top nine. One by one we would find out our destiny.

Doing the calculations in my head I knew that I definitely didn't want to be called at 9am. If the phone rang then you would know immediately that you were out. I thought, maybe a few minutes for each of the three conversations with the girls who didn't make the team. So, from about ten past nine onward, I would be safe.

9:05am

I was pacing around the living room of our tiny home, walking so quickly I could have drilled circles in the ground. My nails were gnawed down from the anxiety. My stomach was flip-flopping from nerves. I wanted to lie down from the extreme exhaustion that my body was feeling but my limbs were being pumped with stress and adrenaline. Lexi was patiently sitting on the couch trying to calm me down. But there was nothing to say that would stop how I felt. There were no words. Just waiting.

9:08am

The sound I had been waiting for all morning started buzzing from my phone lying on the bed. I was terrified to look to see who was calling but we both know who it would be. Brian.

This was it. But it was too soon. There was no way that he could've gotten through all of the calls already! My stomach dropped. Shit. I didn't make it. I knew it. There was no way.

Feeling defeated already, I reluctantly picked up the phone. "Hello?" I forced the words out. My hands were trembling. My lip was quivering. Tears were pooling in my eyes ready to spill over the brim in what I thought would be utter despair.

"Hi Danielle, this is Brian. I just wanted to tell you that-"

I felt like I was going to break into a million pieces from complete and utter fear of what I thought the following words would be. But I was wrong.

"Of course you made team. You are going to the Olympics. Congratulations, love. Now I have a few more people that I have to call so if you don't mind, I have to go."

As if a dam of emotion exploded from inside me, my eyes flooded with tears. Relief. Euphoria. Bliss. Shock. Disbelief. Gratitude. Every emotion poured through me.

"Thank you," was all I was able to mutter through the sobs. "Thank you, Brian, thank you!"

My entire body was vibrating as I let all the emotion rush through me. Hot tears were cascading down my face, springing from the core of my soul. The little girl who struggled with confidence. The teenager who never felt she properly fit in the team. The young adult who knew there was something great out there for her somewhere, someday, but wasn't sure how to go about it. The twenty-one-year-old concussed girl who had a flame ignited inside her at the hope of an opportunity. The relentlessly optimistic and hardworking young woman who gave up everything to move across to world to pursue an impossible dream, She did it. I did it!

Every fear that I leapt into was worth it. Every worry that knotted my stomach was defeated. Every time my heart ached from missing my family, from being so far from my friends, from feeling so alone – was worth it. Every morning I forced my aching exhausted body out of bed to walk head-first into another day of training was worth it. Every single moment of financial stress was worth it. Every single second that my lungs wanted to burst, my brain wanted to give up and my heart felt like it was going to explode pushing myself to the extreme limit at training in the pursuit of improvement, was worth it.

My soul was exploding with love, pride, joy and most of all – gratitude.

I was going to the Olympics. I was going to become an Olympian.

We all have those moments in our lives. Yes, you may not have gotten the call that you have made the Olympic team, of course. But a moment of pure, absolute, boundless joy. Joy that is so beautiful it makes you feel like your soul is shining. Maybe that moment was yesterday, last week or last year.

No matter the journey that your life has led you on, where you come from or what your upbringing was like – I know ALL of us have at least ONE of those moments.

Tap into that feeling in that moment. Let the corners of your mouth curl up into a smile and your eyes shine bright from bliss.

Thinking about that moment it's hard to not see how flipping beautiful life can be when we take a moment to FEEL.

Looking back in that moment when you were nourishing yourself with love and gratitude for the moment, do you notice how PRESENT you were?

You allowed yourself to be so fully absorbed in THAT exact moment that NOTHING else seemed to matter. The beauty of the past crashed on the shore of the future as you absorbed the ocean mist that exits in the present. Fears weren't even a passing thought in your brain because you just were. You were just existing in the power of...

▶ PRESENCE

❯ **How often in your life do you give yourself the space to exist in the present?**

❯ **How often do you let go of the past and the future and exist in the moment?**

❯ **How often do you look around at everything in your vicinity and truly soak in the beauty of it in that moment?**

As a society we are so CONDITIONED to bypass presence in our life. We are all living in this world that is becoming so fast-paced. There is ALWAYS something to do to entertain us. If we don't spend our days rushing from one thing to another, then we become bored. And in boredom we try to fill that void with something artificial, usually our personal vice – food, alcohol, drugs, tv, social media. Whatever it is, we are conditioned to not ever really allowing ourselves to sit alone with our happy thoughts.

Think about it – even in the moments when we could have a second of space – like simply waiting in line for a coffee– what do we all do? Fill.

Pick up our phones, pull out our computer, turn on the TV, grab a crappy magazine, turn on a podcast, listen to music. And if we don't? And we allow ourselves to be that one person that isn't 85 years old and we happily sit, waiting and allow ourselves to be present – we look absolutely bonkers! Right?

Now, please know that I am not higher than thou. I don't sit here saying that we all need to throw out our phones, get rid of our TVs, take away our podcasts and just all walk around absorbing every passing moment in bliss. Look, I think that if that happened the world would be a pretty darn peaceful place, but I do have a touch of realism in my life.

However I also think that we all need to allow more moments of presence in our lives where we allow ourselves to sit back and take in the beauty that is around us. Because only in moments of true presence can we truly feel the tsunami of gratitude. And that combination of gratitude and presence combines together to create pure...

HAPPINESS.

Now I know I can get a little bit wrapped up in the rainbows, sunshine and magic that is being thankful – but let me tell you, beautiful amigos...

Being thankful for everyday on the journey to "achieving" your dreams is essential.

Yes, you may not be where you want to be yet.

Yes, you may have a long way to go, in your mind.

Yes, you may have a lot of hard work ahead of you.

Yes, you may be swatting through some adversity.

Yes, you may feel a bit lost as to what is your next move.

But if you are

1. **CLEAR** on your **LIMITING SELF-BELIEFS** and know what is holding you back;

2. Doing what you **LOVE** and following your passion;

3. Accepting that **ADVERSITY** is part of the process and aware that it will show its blessing soon enough;

4. Taking the **REQUIRED ACTION** to get where you want to be; and

5. **IMPROVING** yourself along the process;

You are doing it already. You have taken all the right steps and are overcoming the hurdles and doing what you LOVE!

Taking a moment to appreciate the presence of that – you can't help BUT feel happy and grateful.

Give yourself a moment to take it all in because time is so fleeting.

Now that we are all levitating on a magic carpet made of gratitude and presence lets take a moment to be really human and have a little chuckle:

This one is a bit of a doozy, and I am slightly hesitant in sharing it with you, but here goes nothing.

One day, in the lead up to World Champs, our team was training in Perth, in June, which is just creeping up on winter in Australia. Because all homes and buildings in Aus are made to keep everyone cool for summer, during the winter time, unfortunately, it is freezing inside. No one really uses heaters and instead most people just rug up.

On this day we were going to be training outside, so the whole team was decked out in full warmth attire; parkas, sweat pants, jumpers. The whole Aussie nine yards. We were practicing our walk-on outside, beside the length of the pool, to be prepared for the upcoming competition. In synchro, the walk-on is the way the team gets up the stairs and onto the deck to prepare for the routine. It is done in perfect synchronization, like the rest of the swim. In this particular routine, I had to do this bizarre movement and hop from my feet being together to shoulder width apart standing in a partial squat.

This one particular time we were doing it as I hopped I could feel my knees bump my teammates Nikita, who was bending down in front of me, in the bum. Almost as if in slow motion, as soon as I knock her she loses her balance and slowly tips forward, in full clothes, runners, parka and all into the pool, while all of us stand there and watch it all unfold in front of our eyes. Normally, you would be worried about the person in the water's swimming ability, however we didn't quite have that problem. So, as soon as all of us processed what happened, we all burst out laughing! Meanwhile Nikita, who is wearing mountains of clothes is struggling to tread water and I feel so horrible, yet find the situation so funny that I stand there in stitches with the rest of the team.

However, I have one little problem. My weak bladder. In the past, like others on occasion I have wet my undies from a bit too much belly laughter, but this time it was different. My body completely betrayed me!

As hard as I tried to control myself, I couldn't stop. A little bit trickled out and then as if I unleashed the doors of a dam, it all flooded out of me. My mind is racing trying to think how I can hide this from my teammates who are still all wrapped up in laughing at the situation, but that dam was FULL let me tell you. Full and smelly. There is no way I could hide this one. So, I thought I might as well be the first person to throw myself under the bus!

In stitches of laughter and half embarrassment I pat one of my teammates and say, "I'm peeing!" Yah, Yah they just laugh it off. "No seriously guys, I peed myself!"

All at once they turn around with a puzzled look on their face. Their gaze went from my eyes, down my leg as they realized my leggings were – saturated. Yup. Saturated. As Nikita is struggling to pull herself out of the pool, my teammates all turn their laughter and point towards me because, as a twenty something year old, not only did I push my teammates in the pool, but I also – yup, I'm going to say it – peed myself.

Unlikely Olympian. Author. Motivational Speaker & last but not least. Peed herself as an adult. DKism

Another reason I was so thankful for my unique journey that had brought me to that point of making the Olympic team is because I knew how fleeting time was.

At 18 years old I walked away from my sport for what I thought at the time would be forever. Being 18 years old, having done synchro for ten years at that time, I saw in the blink of an eye how fast it all went by. It felt like my whole synchro career had flashed by me.

That perspective made me wish I had I could have soaked up every moment a little bit more. And it taught me to cherish all the little moments.

Because, when something flashes you by, you look back and realize that it is the little moments that you miss, not the big ones. The competitions were always great, but the actual practice time is what made up the bulk of my synchro career.

I missed the catching up with my teammates before training, chatting like we hadn't seen each other in months, when we really all saw each other the previous day. The laughter at the side of pool during training, when we would goof off. The feel of feeling so exhausted yet exhilarated after a routine run-through. The feeling of accomplishment after a productive day of training and showering after practice with my teammates and being silly in the changerooms.

The competitions were wonderful, they left me with beautiful memories. But for me, it was the simple things that I missed.

So when I made that Olympic team, I made a vow to myself to be grateful for every single day in the lead-up to Rio. Less than four and a half months until this entire journey was going to be over. I had seen ten years of my synchro career zip by, so I knew that the next few months would fly by in an instant. I woke up every morning – let the reality of my dream flood through me and soak up the precious gratitude of the day.

A couple hours after we found out that each of us had made the team, we received an email with our ranking. One through twelve. I was ranked fifth. I thought that my boundless gratitude and pride couldn't expand anymore but it did. Not only had I made the team, but I made it fair and square. Safely! I hadn't just skimmed my way in. I didn't come in 8th or 9th.

I was fifth. I was safe. I one thousand percent deserved MY spot.

In that same email, as I was skimming down the names, I saw Cassie was 12th. She didn't make it.

Although I knew deep-down that this would be the case, a wave of relief washed over me. I was heartbroken for her, because I knew how much this would hurt her, but I was also relieved to be able to let her go. To be able to move on and enjoy the journey ahead of me without feeling like I was walking on egg shells in a difficult friendship situation.

It felt like our journey as friends had finally come to an end. As much as the history of our friendship made me want to call her up, go over to her house and console her through her heartbreak – I knew that I couldn't.

I was probably the last person she wanted to see. What is so bizarre about the Olympic Team trial process is that the announcement of the team is the BEST day of your life for some athletes and the WORST day for others. It is selfish, but I knew that I had worked so damn hard to get myself to that point that I deserved to celebrate it and wrap myself up in the fruits of my labor.

The day after our collision in our tech team swim one of my teammates told me about a breakfast conversation that she had with Cassie. It was a comment that broke my heart but also lit a fire in me to stand up for myself. It was a moment, similar to when I refused to apologize – when I had felt like I found my sweet spot in the balance of my self-awareness. I was able to take-on feedback, but I was also able to stand strong in the KNOWLEDGE of who I was.

Cassie said, "If I don't make the team because of what DK did to me, I will resent her for the rest of my life."

Ouch.

More than anything though it broke my heart for her. It made me want to send her love. I KNOW I didn't "do" anything to her because it was a complete accident. The choice to live in resentment for the rest of your life is a toxic place to be.

I could've said the same back in order to play the victim, dove to her level and said the same about her. But that doesn't feel good or cultivate happiness.

So – I chose to forgive her and forgive myself.

If you are a human being reading this, I bet you haven't lived your life unscathed. You have probably hurt and been hurt.. Whatever the circumstance I bet there has been someone at some time that has unintentionally or purposefully caused you deep pain. Or maybe you did it to them.

Those are the adversities of life.

But remember –

> our biggest adversities can be our biggest blessings when we choose to learn from them.

Holding on to that toxicity, that anger, that rage inside you that just wants revenge for the way someone has made you feel will

ONLY deplete your life. Having an intention for revenge will hurt YOU more than it will EVER hurt the person who is the target of your revenge.

> "Resentment is like drinking poison and waiting for the other person to die."
> — Carrie Fisher

Forgiveness is powerful. In my heart I needed to let go of Cassie by forgiving her and move on We were both not benefiting each other's lives anymore.

So, I consciously chose gratitude & forgiveness. I recognized all the beauty she had given me, admitted my wrongs and allowed myself to move on. I broke us up. And it killed me – but I knew it was for the best for us both.

So, I wrote it down and let it go –

Cas;

I just wanted to address the obvious because I hate awkward situations and I know I can be awkward in them. I want to say I am really truly sorry about the difficult situation you are going through. I can't even imagine the heartbreak you are feeling and seeing you the other day I could definitely feel a little bit of it.

I think there's been many stages to our relationship so far, but one definitely was our amazing pre-Australia adventures. I still think back to that day in Vancouver when we ran to each other through the street and embraced in the middle of downtown.

ALONG with our amazing euro trip with the four musketeers. We brought each other so much happiness we got in even more shenanigans and had so much fun. I truly look back on all of those amazing memories and smile, and I always will. We were each other's Rock and partner in crime for quite a while. It was unreal. You helped me through so much with my concussion when I would call you in Montreal sobbing from being so unhappy and frustrated. And I tried my best to help you through your boy troubles and heartbreak. I will always remember that unreal 20th birthday in Montreal getting drunk and silly beyond belief. It was truly a beautiful friendship for the history books.

And then we moved to Australia, and a different stage began. Maybe the move, the stress of synchro, us just growing up in different directions or everything put together, but we changed, and we struggled. Nasty things were said and done, and I know I've said things I'm not proud of and probably vice versa. Our relationship as friends clashed with our relationship as athletes and teammates and in the end our friendship suffered. I think there's no denying that our best friendship slowly turned into more of a 'teammate-ship.' We had moments and glimmers of that amazing thing we'd had before, but for whatever reason it was ultimately different. Maybe you saw it another way, but that's what I truly felt.

There's really no formula or guide book for everything we have gone through together so it's hard to know where to go from here. I'm going to be honest and just say that we haven't been that same level and friends for a long while now. Through this process I had to focus on myself if I wanted to achieve my goals and through that I couldn't be that person for you anymore. Additionally, I have been hurt very deeply by things that you've said and done, as well as the things that happened between us. I was an amazing friend to you because I wanted to be, and I loved it. But now I know I just can't be that friend for you anymore and I believe I detached myself emotionally a while ago because I couldn't deal with the hurt anymore.

But nevertheless, I just want you to know from the bottom of my heart, I truly wish you all the very best in life and love. I have complete confidence that your tenacity and determination will lead you to amazing things in this world. I want you to succeed in everything, but my want doesn't really matter because I KNOW that you will. The next little while might be a little different than you planned but I know you have the right tools and the right people surrounding you to get you strongly back on your feet.

At the moment, with everything in the past and now in the present, it is difficult to be friends, maybe someday in the future we will get that back, but I know it's not there right now. With the beautiful friendship that we had, my platonic love and best wishes for you will always be there. Ultimately I just want you to know that I do love you and wish you everything good in this world.

All the best in everything,

And lots of love from the bottom of my heart,

DK

Maybe on the journey of your dream there isn't anyone or anything to let go of. To live in true thankfulness and gratitude we need to release ourselves of any toxicity, anger and negative emotions that are holding us back.

Maybe that anger is towards a situation or a person. Maybe it is towards ourselves for what we have done in the past.

So I ask you, I challenge you:

- **Is there anyone you have to forgive on your journey to exist in full gratitude?**

- **Is there a past situation that is holding you back from existing in that highest pure vibration of love?**

- **Is it you that you need to forgive?**

Write it down. Flush it out. Get out all the pain. All the anger. All the angst and toxicity inside you that doesn't feel good. Put it on a piece of paper. And...

Burn it.

In a safe place. A sink, a fireplace or somewhere outdoors. Allow the words to turn to ashes and return to the ground. Watch the pain burn away as it goes back to the earth where it is from. With each morsel of paper that transforms, feel yourself letting go of everything that is holding you back from that pure love, gratitude and presence that exists in us all.

In writing this book I had a lot of hesitation as to whether or not I should include all the events with Cassie. I hope I have done my best to not do that. I can only be responsible for my own actions in this lifetime and I want to live with as much love and kindness as I can, while also standing in my truth. I chose to write about it because I believe it is a big part of me finding my truth and I want to give you the honest version of the story.

At the end of the day though, I want you to know that Cas is a beautiful person. She served as one of my best friends for an important chunk of my life. For many years she was an amazing friend and a gorgeous human being. She had her vices, as we all do. And I believe those vices held her back from living as the most true and beautiful version of herself which I saw as her best friend. Cassie was only doing the best she could with what she had. Just like Lisa, just like Julie. I believe that all human beings are just doing their best.

I am grateful for everything Cas gave me; a few beautiful years of friendship, an opportunity of a lifetime to go after a dream together, so many precious memories filled with laughter and tears, and one of my most valuable lessons in life in learning to stand up for myself and step into the power of who I am.

After finding out the Olympic team we barely got a moment to breathe before we had to jump right back into the game. The morning of April 8th we all showed up to the pool in emotionally exhausted bodies but with so much eagerness for what was to come.

Life for the next few months was a treadmill of excitement. We were pretty much travelling non-stop, fly-in fly-out nomads. Never staying in one place for more than a couple weeks at a time. We had so many unreal experiences lined up for us in the coming months that we really only focused on one day at a time.

We spent a week in Perth after Olympic team trials, training hard and pulling together our routine before we got to become VIP guests on a once-in-a-lifetime trip with one of the world's richest ladies.

Don't get me wrong, being an athlete is a lot of damn hard work. But there are definitely perks. For us one of those perks was Synchro Australia's biggest fan, greatest supporter and true guardian Angel – Australia's richest women – Mrs. Gina Rinehart.

Mrs. Rinehart became a sponsor of Synchro Australia in 2015. Being an advocate for powerful women in Australia and a lover of swimming, her company Hancock Prospecting, jumped on board to support us in the lead up to the Olympic Games. Mrs. Rinehart, needless to say, became enamored with us and we were endlessly grateful for her and her companies support.

Her support literally saved us. Hancock Prospecting's sponsorship for Synchro Australia only left us with about a $20k bill to be on the Olympic team in 2016. It boggles my mind to think what it would have been without her help.

So, a week after our team was announced, we were whisked away to what felt like a parallel universe. Red dirt, sky-rocketing temperatures, the middle of nowhere in Western Australia – Roy Hill Iron Ore Mine.

Mrs. Rinehart made her fortune in iron ore mining. A business that was passed down from her late father Lang Hancock. After Mr. Hancock spotted the iron ore deposits in the early 1960s it took decades for the family's privately-owned mine to get up and running.

At the time, we had no idea what we were walking in to. Our lives were not our own anymore. For the next six months, our schedule and lives were in the hands of Synchro Australia and the Australian Olympic Committee. So, going up to the mine we truly had no idea what to expect. But it was like nothing else.

We flew up and were treated like stars. A VIP bus was waiting for us, there were gift bags on our seats, we were given executive suites at the mine site and a news camera crew following us around. We were all struggling athletes who had to pinch pennies to pay for food and rent, yet all of a sudden, we were in a different light. It was our first taste of being "Olympians."

We were whisked around the mine, brought back to the village to perform for all the workers before we were treated to a dinner under the stars in the executive area. It felt like a constant 'pinch me' moment. The continuous limiting self-belief's filing into my mind thinking "Who the heck am I to be here? Having dinner beside a billionaire, across the table from the company's CEO, having casual conversation about mining deals?"

The next morning we were treated to a buffet breakfast by a local creek before we were off to our next location for the weekend. Uluru. Via private jet. To meet up with the recently selected Aussie Olympic swimmers. For another beautiful dinner under the stars.

In moments like that, it can be quite easy to find gratitude. And presence flows, knowing that all those moments were so fleeting.

Mrs. Rinehart being a relatively public figure in Australia, people quite often ask me what she is like. How she acts and what I think of her.

In my one hundred percent truth I only have good things to say about her. We have been blessed to have been invited to multiple events and private dinners with her. Every time I have spent time with her she has been nothing but lovely, generous and kind to me. I only choose to judge people on how I have been treated by them personally, and I believe she truly is a powerful yet generous and kind women. For goodness sake, she took us on her private plane and walked around in bare feet personally serving us beverages. Worth over five billion dollars and she is serving little old me a ginger beer.

> Meanwhile, the next day my $900 car broke down on the side of the highway and I could barely afford to get it towed. Now that's a darn parallel universe for you.

▸ KNOWING YOUR DREAM

The beauty of all those experiences taught me an invaluable lesson. Mrs. Rinehart lives what our societal culture might token – the "dream". People may see her as "successful," "prosperous," or "winning at the game of life."

She has done what the movies show as the story book ending. Work hard and make millions. Sorry, billions. To be honest, I can't even really comprehend what billions even look like.

Seeing the fruits of that labor, the mine site, the plane, the beautiful dinners, the lavish luxuries it would be easy for me to be entranced by those things and transfer them to being my own desires. Take it on as my own dream. Believe that what she has is what I want too.

But that would be, as one of my personal role models, conscious AF guru's Peta Kelly says in her book "Earth is Hiring" – a

BORROWED DREAM.

A borrowed dream is a dream that you have copied from someone else and tried to paste into your future. You think that it sounds good so that is what you want too, you think that because someone you admire did it that you should go after that too. Right? Wrong.

I have had the honor and privilege to go into schools and share my story with school children. I love sharing with them the power of working hard, leaping into their fear, doing what they love and going after their dream. But I am always very cautious and hesitant when I hear kids afterwards come up to me and say that now – "I want to go to the Olympics too!"

It makes me squirm a bit on the inside in fear that maybe I have misled them. It is something I am working on and will change for the future. But I don't want them to borrow my dream. I want them to write their own.

It is easy to get inspired by someone's journey and think – I WANT TO DO THAT TOO!

Maybe you do. Maybe it has been something that you always wanted to do and in your core it feels good. But it is SO important to tap into that self-awareness inside, tap into truth that is inside of you. Your own personal inner knowing.

Because, if we go down the path of a borrowed dream, the universe will try to realign us. Things will happen, stuff will go wrong, it won't FEEL good. Something will be off.

In the formulation of working through working smarter, you should massage out the knots that don't serve you, the goals that aren't yours and the desires you have copied from someone else.

It goes for EVERYTHING as well – not just dreams. We can be INSPIRED by others but through our self-awareness we must weed out what is for us and what is not.

Just because someone else started their own business and went on Shark Tank doesn't mean that has to be your goal to. Just because someone else got the "body of their dreams" through a fitness competition, doesn't mean you have to do one too. Just because someone else uprooted their life to live in Bali doesn't mean you should too. Just because someone else home-schooled their kids doesn't mean you should too. Just because someone else became a teacher because they adore children doesn't mean you should too. Just because someone else became a billionaire through mining and lives a lavish lifestyle doesn't mean you have to too.

Do what is right FOR YOU.

Do what feels good to YOU.

Do what is truth for YOU.

Do what feels in alignment FOR YOU.

Not for Tom or Sally or Susan down the road, for you.

And how does gratitude and presence tie into all of this, you may ask?

Because it is so much harder for gratitude and presence and prosperity and abundance to flow when you are living in someone else's dream.

Sometimes, to figure that out takes a little bit of trial and error. That's okay keep on cycling forward up the beautiful path that is your life's purpose.

There was a fast fall for coming down from living the high life with Mrs. R. After Uluru she and her elite guests, with the Olympic Swimmers and beach volleyball players headed to Sydney to finish the tour with a celebratory yacht party in Sydney Harbor. Meanwhile, we had to get back to Perth to get to work. We had one week until we were leaving for our first competition as an Olympic team in Tokyo, Japan.

As a team we were on an interesting ride. We knew that we weren't medal contenders at the Olympics. Not even close. That wasn't being pessimistic or negative but just living in the reality of the situation.

Being a judged sport, the world ranking in synchro is hard to crack. Quite often countries are in similar spots from year to year. It takes years upon years for a country to truly move up the rankings in our sport. As well, it is extremely hard to get past some of the top countries; Russia, Japan, China and Ukraine. They all have fully-funded programs. All the swimmers are paid, full-time athletes. They have a staff of physios and massage therapists who travel around with them. They don't have to stress about how they are going to work to pay for life at the end of training day. Especially in countries like Russia and China, synchro isn't just a sport, it is national treasure.

Children are picked from a young age to join sports schools based on their body type fitting the ideal synchro swimmer physique. As they grow up, they train and go to school at the same time. They are molded into the "perfect" athlete. By the time they get to the elite level, the national team literally has hundreds of almost identical athletes to choose from to make up a team of the best eight. It is a different world from what it is like in Australia. Even Canada. Both countries can't compete with that culture. It wouldn't be accepted here.

I have spent a long time thinking about it as well. For my own life, I wouldn't want that. I don't know if those athletes are truly happy or not, I can't speak for them. But I truly appreciate the balance that I have had in my life. I am grateful that as much as synchro was a massive part of me I still have the ability to do other things, have other interests and try other sports.

I greatly respect the discipline those countries have, but I am okay with not being in the top-ranking countries in the world, yet still having balance in my life overall.

So, going into the Olympic games we knew we weren't coming in the top half. We were fighting for 7th. Yes, I know what you are thinking, seven out of eight? Yes.

So that meant we had to take down our biggest competitor, Egypt. The top country in the next continent where the popularity of synchro was lower than the rest of the world, Africa.

The Japan Open went well for us for our first competition. Coming together as an Olympic team for the first time was liberating. After months of competing against each other to fight for our spots we finally had the chance to unite ourselves. Bind together and be stronger as one.

Although the team was a different assortment than we all predicted before trials, we came together perfectly. All of us gelled really well together. The nine of us were fully dedicated to each other, to our goals and to our country. We all knew we weren't fighting for podium. We were fighting for seventh, but more importantly than that, we were fighting to be the best that we could be at the Olympic Games.

▸ WRITING IT DOWN

In all those precious moments leading up to the games, like I said, I made sure to treasure every fleeting moment. I did my best to live in gratitude every single day.

I would wake up in the morning and say in my head the things I was grateful for before I let my feet touch the floor. For just a moment I would sit in stillness to allow myself to soak in the moment and remind myself that I was existing in the dream that I had worked for for so long.

There would be days where I would forget, being too frazzled or tired . Some days I would be nervous to go to training, knowing the blood, sweat and tears that I had to put into the day ahead.

But at the end of the day, when I put my head on that pillow I would be so damn grateful for the life I was living. Because I was pursuing my passion with my absolute synchro soul sisters.

I knew how fleeting time was, so I made sure to record as much as I could. Not only would I write down my daily goals, but I would also record how I was feeling.

I know that not everyone is a writer. We don't all need to write books and record our lives. But no matter if you are good with words or not, I challenge you to write every once in a while. It doesn't have to be every day or even every week, but just whenever your heart is called. Get out a pen and a note book or turn on a computer, open a Word document and allow your mind to flow.

Slowly, that mind will tap into your heart. And your heart will flow onto the page in front of you.

Write without:

- ❯ **judgement.**
- ❯ **structure.**
- ❯ **giving yourself the constraints of time, space or neatness.**
- ❯ **hesitation.**
- ❯ **thinking of speaking to anyone else but your true self.**

Not only is writing therapeutic, allowing those emotions to flow and feel through the healing process. But it also is the story of your life in words. Something to look back on as memory fades to see where you were in that moment. Standing in the truth of who you are in that moment.

Those words capture a small piece of the fleeting time that is life and hold it in a pocket of love for you to look back on with gratitude in the future. Before you know it, your 'now' will become your 'then' and you will look back, wishing to grasp every passing second.

In what seemed like the blink of an eye, April turned to May, May to June and then July. The anticipation inside each and every one of us was boiling to the surface. We were like a simmering pot of excitement, just dying to burst into the Olympic Games. Each moment was like its own precious gem stone of excitement. Being announced as the Olympic Team. Getting our official Qantas tickets, getting our two suitcases of Olympic luggage.

But finally it all came to fruition when, on August 1st, we left Australia behind for the last time as athletes, knowing that we were going to return as Olympians.

It is a funny little bubble you live in when you go to the Olympic games, because it seems as if, at that time, there is nothing else going on in the world except for what is in your immediate existence.

Going through the airport in Sydney on the way to Rio, one of the security guards asked innocently why we were all wearing matching uniforms. To me it seemed quite obvious. We were wearing Olympic uniforms that said Rio Olympics on them. But I kindly told him, in response, that we were the Australian Synchronized Swimming Team, on our way to the Olympic Games.

His response, "Oh, is the Olympics coming up? I had no idea."

In my head I felt shocked! It seemed like anyone who consumed any type of modern technology would have seen the advertisements plastered left and right. Not to mention the physical ads everywhere from bus stops to billboards. How could you NOT know the Olympics is coming up?

That was definitely a reality check.

When we get so wrapped up in our own vision and dream it can sometimes seem ridiculous if others don't get it too. If they don't care so passionately and deeply about the same thing we do.

How could someone not care about saving the turtles? Or diminishing their plastic usage for the ocean? How could someone not know about the importance of a morning routine? Or fueling yourself with healthy food to rejuvenate your health? It may seem crazy that someone doesn't understand the power of balancing your finances to optimize your savings and your wealth?!

Remember to be kind. Be compassionate and know that everyone is on a different chapter in their life. Not everyone is MEANT to be as burning with desire as you to go after their dreams. And a hard one for even me to swallow is that not everyone cares about existing within their ideal life.

In the journey of achieving my next impossible dream to inspire the world to go after theirs, I have to remind myself that NOT everyone is going to see it the way I see it. Just because I care so passionately doesn't mean that everyone else is also going to want to dream big and attain the unlikely and go after their impossible.

Maybe their dream is to be financially stable, pay off their mortgage and live a simple life. If that makes them happy, truly happy at their core. That is enough.

I know - that when we all tap into our true higher selves and align with the true visions for our lives, that we have the power to collectively uplift this world through our consciousness. For Bob or Susan down the road who is doing their job day to day and being kind, compassionate and loving to the people around them and the world is enough.

It is okay to desire more, but it is also okay for others to desire less. Or different. See things in a shifted perspective. We are ALL on our own journey, our job is not to compare our road to others' or judge others for not seeing things from our perspective. Our job is to focus on ourselves. What lights us up and DO it with love. Pursue it with passion. Be clear on what we want, declare it to the world. Know that learning is a constant on the journey and adversity will always inch its way through. And when we are existing in alignment with the power of our true dream, we cannot go wrong.

When you live your life looking forward to a certain date, event or experience for so long – when it actually comes and plays out it can be different from how you have built it up in your mind.

Has that ever happened to you? You are looking forward to something for so damn long and, when it actually plays out, it is so different from what we pictured. Then, when it doesn't play out like we thought, a little INKLING of a feeling pops in. We feel bad about it, but it is - disappointment.

The final and MOST important steps in going after our dreams and manifesting our future reality is...

LETTING GO OF EXPECTATION.

I know, I know, friend – you're like – "DK you're confusing me! I am working towards this massive thing! How can I let go of the expectation of what it will become! Isn't that silly? Isn't that letting go of too much control?"

Stay with me, beautiful people.

It can be hard, but we need to ALLOW our dreams to have a little space. We need to plant the seed, do all the right steps to make it grow. And then LET it grow as it may.

Because we CANNOT completely control the future. To a certain level it is out of our hands. It is up to the universe, God, creator, source, mother nature, fate or whoever you chose to believe in.

We need to provide her with the instructions, follow the steps and let go of what we THINK it will be and love what it is because, when we are in the right head space, I PROMISE YOU – it will be exactly how it is meant to be.

When we let go of the future restrictions that we THINK about how it is going to be – we allow ourselves to come back to the moment and appreciate its beauty in the...

PRESENT.

Expectation is non-presence. It is letting our mind go on a tangent in some imagined future that we have created, when all we can actual control is the present moment. And when we are TRULY existing in the presence, we can have nothing but love and gratitude.

> Touching down in Rio I had all these different expectations of what I thought the following few weeks would be like. In our preparation for the games we got the chance to sit down with other Olympians who had participated in previous games and ask them all about their experiences. They told us what they learnt, how they found it and we listened to what advice they had to give us.
>
> Don't get me wrong, I was bubbling with excitement for every moment. But it was also different from what I had imagined. What I learnt is that that is okay. It works out EXACTLY the way it is meant to. When we realize that – we allow ourselves to exist in the presence, beauty and abundance of what is.
>
> Flying into an Olympic Games is like nothing else I have ever experienced. The pure level of organization on an epic scale is

fascinating to experience. You almost become just a puppet in a show being pushed from one system to the next, flowing through.

As soon as we got off the plane we were filed into a different, special Olympic express lane. We got a special stamp on our passports with the rings on it. When we got to the baggage carousel, all our identical baggage was lined up for us to claim before we were ushered out to a delegate waiting for us to put us on a special bus to take us to the village.

Everything felt like an overload of stimuli. Everywhere you looked there was Olympic branding. Sponsorship posters. Mascots. Not to mention that it was also my first time in South America. So, driving down the freeway on the way to the Olympic Village, seeing all the lush rolling mountains of Rio that were supported by the favelas escalating their way up the mountains, took my breath away.

When we got to the actual Village, it felt like another world. The thirty-odd apartment buildings housing the athletes were all stacked eighteen stories high. Flags of all the world's countries were draped down the sides, proudly bearing their countries' colors. Everywhere you looked you could identify where people were from. Everyone walked around the village wearing their uniform, patriotically proclaiming the name of their country.

All of that, wrapped around by some of the world's highest security. You can imagine it needs to be extremely secure when you have thousands of the world's best athletes, some celebrities and important delegates all in one place. The Village perimeter was surrounded by a tall barbed-wire fence. Beyond the fence was a further perimeter, guarded by the Brazilian police, only allowing certain accredited vehicles within the vicinity. To get in and out of the Village you needed special accreditation and had to go through airport-like security. They ran a tight ship.

It felt kind of like being in a prison. I know that sounds a bit bizarre. But the coolest prison ever and one you REALLY wanted to be in. But a prison nonetheless. However, the entire time I felt nothing less than completely and totally safe.

I was told that quite often, when athletes entered the village for the first time, they would get an overwhelming rush of emotions. Joy. Pride. Gratitude and disbelief. Oddly enough, when we walked into the village for the first time, I felt nothing. That led to a small inkling of disappointment because of my expectation. That was one of my first lessons in learning to let go.

Instead, as soon as we walked through security and out into the open village with sky-high buildings, waving flags and thirty thousand other people, I felt an overwhelming sense of being completely average.

Ironic, I know. I stepped into the Olympic village and felt average!

We had just come from Australia where I was one of 422 people going to one of the most elite events in the world. Just 422 out of a population of 25 million. Despite the interaction with the one security guard in the airport, I am not going to lie, I did feel a bit like royalty leaving Australia.

But then I was chucked into the Olympic village. I was one Olympian in a sea of eleven thousand Olympians! Not only that, but we were at the bottom of the food chain. We weren't gold medalists, celebrities, multi-time Olympians. We were at our first Olympics in a sea of people who were also achieving their dream. It was bizarre, unexpected and completely humbling.

What surprised me most about the entire experience overall was how "normal" it all felt. I know that sounds absolutely crazy. I was at the Olympics, achieving my impossible dream and it felt – normal. Because it had to.

If I, if our team, lived every single day in absolute awe and amazement at where we were living, we wouldn't have been able to stay focused. We had to make every day feel like our new normal. It had to be normal that we woke up every day and dressed ourselves in full Aussie gear where we would then walk and have our every meal in a cafeteria the size of two football stadiums. It had to feel normal that we were coexisting amongst the world's best athletes and constantly saw people walking around with gold medals draped around their necks. It had to feel normal that we were training every day in a pool with other elite synchro Olympians and divers. That normalcy kept us focused on the task at hand. Because truly, we weren't there to experience only the magic of the Olympics. We were there to do a job to be best we could for our country and do the best that we could for ourselves.

What I think many people don't realize when they watch the Olympic games on their TV at home is that when all those athletes are competing and experiencing their life's highs and lows, winning medals and losing to competitors – the majority of athletes are doing what they do every day. Train.

Wake up, eat, train, recover, eat, repeat. When you are finished, the partying comes and the celebration ensues – but for the most part, you have to live your normal routine within the bizarre and beautiful emotionally heightened Olympic bubble.

And that is what we did. Wake up, walk to the cafeteria, take the bus to training for about six hours, come back, recover, watch a few events on TV and repeat. Again, that is where a little bit of the disappointment can flow in when you live in a state of expectation. Keep in mind as well that we were competing in the last few days of the games, so from the day we arrived before the Opening Ceremony we still had about two weeks to go.

It took me a bit of time to settle into that feeling of normalcy. But, when I finally did, it gave me the presence and insight to find the beauty in the little moments. I began to hold onto the precious daily experiences that felt normal, but I knew that I would look back at it all with a grin from ear to ear.

One of those little moments was in the cafeteria on just another day of training. I was walking in behind a tiny little athlete from Argentina. As she was moving towards a table of friends from all different countries they all pushed back their chairs, stood up and started clapping for her. She stopped in her tracks. Put her hand on her heart and tears started flowing down her face. I didn't know who she was, what sport she did, but I knew from that reaction that she had just won a medal for her country. A medal in her sport and her fellow competitors from around the world were applauding her with complete and total respect.

That moment took my breath away. I stood there, as an outsider looking in on that situation that to me, showed the absolute pure beauty that is the Olympic Games. For me that is what the Olympics is about. My devoted belief in the beauty of love and the power of unity. I was seeing that in front of my eyes. For me the Olympic Games is more than just the world's grandest sporting event. It is a metaphor for the potential in all of us when we work hard for something we believe in, do what we love and come together as a world. As people, countries and a planet we put down our differences and take the chance to be our best selves. To perform at our peak and reach our potential. It's about supporting one another, in the good times and in the bad. In the moments when no one is watching and the other moments when the world's eyes are on you and the pressure is on your shoulders.

That moment, with the Argentinian athlete, brought it all together for me.

That moment is one that I hold dear in my heart. One I could never have **expected,** but found when I let go of the attachment of what I thought would be and lived in the beauty of what **IS.**

One of the benefits of competing at the end of the Games was that we got the opportunity to walk in the Opening Ceremony. What many people don't know, is that lots of athletes don't actually get the chance to experience the Opening Ceremony at an Olympics because of the magnitude and effort of the entire event. Many athletes watch it in their countries' buildings from the Village. So a lot of the people you see walking in with the countries are the team of staff and coaches who support all the athletes.

On the day of the Opening Ceremony all athletes who are attending are told to be ready, fully dressed in their specific opening ceremony outfits, outside the building by 5pm. It takes about three hours to get the thousands of athletes to file through the Village into busses down the freeway to Maracanã Arena to walk into the world's greatest show. The evening is a combination of sparkling excitement weaved through with long periods of waiting. But none of us cared, because we were all trying to soak in every passing moment.

I was doing everything I could to not let myself get too excited. But I truly felt like I was living in a dream that was my real true life. For that evening I allowed myself to let down the walls I had been holding up to maintain my focus and I allowed the light of the night to shine through.

As soon as we got off the buses we were ushered to the front of the parade while countries in the second half of the alphabet were put in a waiting arena nearby. The closer we got to the arena, the more and more excruciating the waiting was. It felt like we were moving at a sloth-like place.

Dancers, volunteers and performers were walking by us in crazy costumes as we, not so patiently, waited for our moment. Bursts of light beamed from the top of the open-air arena, synchronized with eruptions of the crowd's roar. My stomach was doing flip-flops while my insides were buzzing. I was doing everything in my will power to not bounce with excitement.

My teammates and I had worked our way to the front of the Aussie team, determined to get on TV and wave to our families around the world. The closer we got to the entrance to the stadium the more excruciating was the waiting. All I wanted to do was sprint through the dark tunnel to the other side, but I was also trying to grasp every passing moment, knowing how fleeting it was.

As our flag-bearer inched her way into the darkness of the tunnel, the light from the other side burst through. It felt like I was walking into heaven. Waiting for a moment that I never thought would be my reality. A moment that I thought only belonged to others who were good enough, who were worthy, who were deserving of being Olympians. Not me, right? But yet, there I was.

As we all shuffled into the darkness of the tunnel I grabbed my teammate Emily's hand. I squeezed it so tight and couldn't let go. I felt like I needed the emotional support. That maybe the physical touch of her palm in mine to remind me that this wasn't a dream, it was real life.

I was looking around in complete amazement. Taking in every sound, every scent, every breath. Existing in complete and total presence.

A lump started to work its way up my throat. I was so used to this lump being associated with fear. But this lump was different. This lump was a bomb of emotion. As if it had a slow release within me that bomb triggered tears to well in my eyes that blurred my vision as it finally hit me.

I did it!

In releasing my expectation and living in the present I was gifted with the overwhelming beauty of elation beyond what I have ever known, love greater than I have ever expected and pride pulsing through me more powerful than I knew existed.

I had made it to the Olympic Games.

As if on cue, an Aussie voice from the crowd behind me bellowed, "Aussie, Aussie, Aussie"!

A call that for so long I struggled to identify with. A chant that I loved but I felt like a traitor responding to because I didn't sound like the rest. But then I was reminded of the blood of my heritage that pulsed through the heartbeat of my ancestors. The patriotism of my grandfathers fighting for Australia in the war. I knew that my accent didn't affect my love for this country that I now call my home. No one could take away the burning passion of love that I have for Australia. I knew that I belong here, I deserve to be on this team, and I am Aussie.

So, with my Canadian accent, without a hint of hesitation, I joined the crowd as I thundered back "Oi, Oi, Oi!"

The tears brimming in my eyes gushed down my face as we continued.

"Aussie, Aussie, Aussie"

"Oi, Oi, Oi"

We chanted over and over and over again. Yelling so loudly my voice was cracking. As I continued to squeeze Emily's hand I pulled my phone out to capture the moment. But nothing would ever be able to capture the beauty of the moment with the buzzing patriotism of the crowd.

I felt like my heart was swelling with pride for my country, my team and pride for myself.

Every tear that flowed down my face felt like an obstacle I had overcome. A hurdle that I had leapt. A limiting self-belief that I had quietened. I was existing in pure natural ecstasy.

As we crept our way closer to the entrance to the arena, I put down my phone, squeezed Em's hand and walked into the light of the stadium.

In that moment, I knew I had become an Olympian.

Each passing moment, for the entire evening, it felt like I had my eyes wide and my mouth open, stunned by the power of the Olympics and the accomplishment that I finally felt like I had achieved. It was magic.

After years of obsessively watching the Olympics Opening Ceremonies on TV in pure elation while all the countries were walking in. There I was, doing it. Doing what was my impossible, my unlikely dream. The unlikely Olympian.

Walking in the Opening Ceremony at the Olympics is one of my most precious memories, because I released myself from the tunnel-vision focused attitude I needed to have. I let go of constantly thinking about how I could optimize my performance to be in my best shape for the competition to exist in the presence, to truly let myself *experience* the moment.

Whenever I explain my Olympic experience to others I get a bit nervous telling them about it all through my perception. People see the Olympics on TV every two to four years and build up their beliefs about what it is like. TV and advertising do a phenomenal job of making it all look like magic from the outside. Every achievement is a glorious celebratory moment and every heartbreak is an emotional montage. I don't want to break down the perception that they have in their minds for what they believe it should be like, but I also want to share the truth of what it all looks like from the inside of the bubble.

The morning after the Opening Ceremony was rough. Although none of us had had a lick of alcohol it felt like we were hung over. By the time the event was over, we all piled into buses and got back to the Village it was three in the morning. On the bus ride home we all sat there in awe, stunned at the magic of what had just happened. Going through all of our pictures, videos and memories we were already living in nostalgia trying to let the experience marinate in our minds.

Waking up that following morning, though, was difficult. The overwhelming emotion of the previous night left us in a hungover state. Exhausted, dehydrated and a bit grumpy. It makes you realize why many athletes who compete at the beginning of the competition don't participate in the Opening Ceremony. When you are existing in an almost prime state, eating clean, training hard and optimizing rest − a feeling like that is very foreign. It took us a few days to recover, but nevertheless, training didn't stop. We got up, dragged ourselves out of bed, ate what we could and made our way to training.

The Opening Ceremony was on August 5th, but we didn't compete until the 18th and 19th of August so we still had ample time before it was our moment. Each day was filled with normality, which was long hours of training. We were existing in this bizarre vortex where we were counting down the days until we were going to compete but also holding onto each passionate moment, trying to take it all in. By that point our training was pretty monotonous. We had our routines down pat – our hour of activation and land drill, thirty-minute warm-up, technical drills, then spending the rest of training time working through our routine. There was nothing more we could change in our routine; it was just maintaining where we were at and getting used to our surroundings.

What I didn't realize until I got to Rio myself is that we actually got the opportunity to train and compete in the competition pool countless times before our actual event. The Maria Lenk Marina, which synchro shared with water polo and diving, had three pools. A 50m competition pool three meters deep, with a dive pool at the end, and another 50m training and water polo pool outside the stadium. Each day, depending on any events competing, we would train with our music in the competition or training pool.

As each day passed and we got closer to our competition date, it was bizarre to feel so normal and comfortable swimming in the pool where in a few days we would have the pinnacle swim of our life. The only difference would be the cameras and people filling the stands, the rest was all existing in the strange normal.

Nevertheless, as life likes to have it, adversity ALWAYS creeps her little way in.

One of those adversities was – swimming in the green pool.

One of my most popular questions I get asked when people hear that I went to the Rio Olympics is asking about the green pool. We were in the stadium with the green pool.

The divers got the short end of the stick having to swim in the worst pool of all. And to be completely honest, in real life it looked worse than on TV. The divers would practice at the same time as us and, as the days went on and the pool got murkier and murkier, eventually you couldn't actually see the athletes as they entered the water!

As their pool got worse we started to notice that the water in our 50m was changing as well. At the beginning of the Games it started off okay, but as each day passed by it would get a little bit murkier, a slight bit greener and a lot colder. Clarity of the water is really important in synchro because when we compete with no goggles we need to be able to see our teammates underwater with our eyes open. When it was at its worst I could barely see my teammates who were less than a meter away from me!

This lesson of adversity took a powerful lean into Brian's phrase – "Control the controllables."

It was annoying, it affected our training, but it was out of our hands. And stressing about something that we couldn't control was only a waste of our energy. We had to get really good at bouncing back from those adversities, do the best we could with what we had to optimize our strengths and let go of everything else. We had to come together as a team and block everything else out.

We heard that they were constantly trying to fix the water, but it only seemed to be getting worse! In all fairness, there are thousands of liters in 50m pool, and it isn't so easy to just instantly change the consistency of the water. The only solution was to empty the pool and refill it, but with athletes constantly training in it from morning to night there wouldn't be enough time. Until there was no other option.

The duets competed their tech and free routines a few days before the teams. Rose and Nikita were the duet for Australia. The morning that we rocked up to the pool to cheer them on – they had finally found a solution. An unconventional one, but none-the-less a solution. When we got to Maria Lenk Arena to go into the athletes' entrance to the stands we saw all these makeshift pipes running from the outdoor pool to the indoor pool.

The organizers had finally decided to drain the murky pool and start afresh but they didn't have enough time to stabilize the chlorine levels with fresh water before the competition started, so they decided to take the water from the outdoor training pool. Cutting it really close, they finished filling up the pool just before the competition warm-up – leaving NO room for errors if anything was wrong. Luckily though, by the time the duets dove into the water, it was absolutely perfect. Rose and Nikita swam beautifully and, watching them in the stands as their teammate, friend and fellow Aussie was one of my greatest honors.

And then it was our turn.

I felt really fortunate that I was in both routines. Tech and Free. For me that meant I got to compete at the Olympics twice. On August 18th & 19th.

I had many different assumptions of what my Olympic swim would be like. As soon as I got that opportunity from Cassie I imagined myself up there on stage. It seemed so impossible, but I could still see it. Until you live it though, you can never truly grasp what it is actually like. Because it is ungraspable.

The morning of both routines I woke up feeling pretty darn normal. After living in the Rio Village for two weeks it honestly just, kind of, felt like another day where we had to swim our routine in the same pool we had been swimming in for a couple weeks, just this time with pretty suits, gelled hair, cameras and a crowd.

I was told that many athletes don't sleep the night before they compete. They are so nervous that they can't get a wink of sleep in. Luckily that wasn't me. That's one of those expectations that works in your favor if it doesn't play out exactly as you think.

As I was packing my bag for the day with all my gel, makeup and suits, it was bizarre to think that in just 24 -48 hours this would all be over. Then what? I couldn't think that far, it scared me. So I remained infinitely present.

On the bus to the pool the nerves started to rise inside me. I started to think about all my family in Rio who were waiting to watch this moment; my Mum and Dad, my two sisters, two brothers, my sister-in-law Jennifer, my beautiful best friend Mara and her Mum, my partner Lexi and his friend Scotty. I had an army of people who had travelled across the world for me. All for these swims.

No pressure, right?

Then I started to think about all my friends and family members around the globe getting ready to tune in. Stopping in the middle of their day, waking up in the middle of the night – all to see a glimpse of me, a glimpse of our team on TV. That thought didn't help the nerves either.

So, as I had learned – I came back to the moment. To the present. It was the only place I could be, because everything else was too much. To be in the best mind frame to perform I had to be present.

The power of presence goes far beyond being integrated into everyday life. With presence comes gratitude but ALSO with presence comes...

> PEAK PERFORMANCE.

As humans, we are so stuck in our conditioned mind, constantly THINKING. Letting our mind wander to the worries of the future and the memories of the past. Those thoughts are important to have at times, of course, but as a society we live in that state too often. And when we're are in our wandering mind we are never as powerful, productive or proactive in the present moment.

Having presence is more than just something set aside for yogis, monks and those who meditate, it is also for athletes.

> Presence is a power that exists in all of us
> if we allow ourselves to tap into our genius.

When athletes are performing at, and preparing for, a high level of competition, presence is key. It takes practice to perform with the pressure of the world on your shoulders and also EXTREME focus. Therefore extreme focus is presence. Before and during the times whenever I compete, my mind is in a constant battle of bringing myself back to presence. I need to remind my brain of what it needs to focus on in the future but also realize that ALL I can control is this exact present moment RIGHT now.

I can set my mind up with the condition for how I want my routine to play out – but once I do that, I bring myself back to the moment. As soon as my brain starts to create all the different possible futures through worry, I am not present. I am not in my prime state.

It's exactly the same when I am competing. In any sport, especially synchro that presence is so damn hard when your body is fighting exhaustion. During a routine all my mind wants to do is wander to the future in a few seconds when my fatigued lungs get to breathe. It is my brain fighting my body. But I constantly work on being in the present moment, focusing on the correct movements in that time and trust that all the work I have done has prepared me for this.

The more you figure out that the human programming of your brain is nowhere near as powerful as the possibility of your mind, our soul through reprograming its processes – you will move closer to your dream. You will overcome those limiting self-beliefs and you will make the most unlikely of things happen.

> Standing there in front of the mirror, slopping on our special synchro gel blend, I felt like I was living someone else's life. There I was, getting ready beside the Russian team, the world's

best team and leaders in synchro, while I was gelling my hair for the final times about to swim in the Olympic Games.

Staring at my body in the reflection, I had completely changed. Not only on the outside, but on the inside as well. I was not the same girl who avoided her reflection, pinched her stomach as she cried in the mirror with self-hatred in her heart; who never believed she would make anything of herself in synchro because she was not the right body type, not flexible, not graceful, not talented – just not enough to ever make anything of herself.

No. I was not her anymore.

I stood there, an elevated version of myself that I had transformed into through hard work. Pushing past my limiting self-beliefs by listening to the whisper inside my soul and taking a leap at an opportunity that I worked my ass off for. And, most importantly, through constantly learning from others and myself on the way.

I saw that girl in the reflection and was proud. After a lifetime of shame for my reflection I finally realized that I was proud of who I was and proud of who I knew I would continue to become.

I stood there looking around at my teammates, all getting ready as we were trying to laugh through our nerves. Girls who were strangers to me only a few short years ago and now were all my closest friends.

Four years earlier I was sitting at home in Vancouver, proudly watching the London 2012 synchro event on TV at home. Watching Canada swim, watching Australia swim. Watching Bianca swim who is now my team captain, and I am the assistant captain! Imagine if I told that girl then where she would be now?! Only three years earlier I was backpacking my way around Europe, struggling with my body image that was a reflection of my drinking lifestyle and my self-hatred. Imagine if I told HER where I would be in a few years' time. It seemed absurd! Unreal! Impossible!

But yet here I was.

As we finished getting ready with our makeup done and our hair in place topped off with our sparkly suits - I brought myself back to the zone.

I left the change room behind knowing that next time I came back I would be someone who had competed at the Olympic Games. I took one last look in the mirror and repeated to myself my new beliefs.

> **I am STRONG**
> **I am CAPABLE**
> **I am CONFIDENT**

Standing there, in the on-call room, waiting for our moments to compete, my body started to feel numb. From nausea and numb from nerves. There was nothing else left in me although I had the constant urge to pee. My body was jumping into fight or flight mode but my mind was pulling me back to the moment. Rewiring the condition of my humanness to optimize my performance.

As we could hear the music of the competitors before us reverberating outside, Bianca brought us all together in a circle and reviewed our focuses for the swim for the last time. We knew the focuses inside-out. We knew the routine inside-out. We knew exactly what we had to do. We just had to do it.

We were ushered out into the hallway as the team before us was swimming. All I wanted to do was run away. I was terrified, but excited. Nervous, but prepared. I wanted it to be over, but I wanted to hold this moment in time. Every emotion possible was pulsing through me. My mind was fighting the urge to think about my family, eagerly sitting in the stands cheering. About my friends around the world. I kept pulling myself back to the present, repeating my affirmations and reminding myself of Bianca's mantra to us, "We've got this, team."

I wouldn't have wanted to be going out there with anyone else. I loved each of my teammates with my whole heart. I trusted them with my life. I knew that they would do what they needed to do for us, for Australia and I would too.

My throat was gulping for salvia as the nerves made my mouth feel as dry as the desert. My limbs felt weak. I thought I was going to pass out, but I knew I would be fine.

The cheers erupted from the crowd just outside as the team before us walked off the stage.

Without a moment to think, the volunteers ushered us to the bottom of the stairs to the stage. We walked with a subtle urgency, trying as hard as we might to keep our nervous system calm in a hyper-real situation. Cameras in our faces and thousands, millions of eyes on us as "Land down under" came on and the announcer proclaimed...

"Australia!"

The biggest moment of our entire lives was now.

Chapter 7

Y – YOU

My Olympic swims were three minutes and four minutes long. About seven minutes in total. Seven minutes that I had my moment to shine on the Olympic stage. Four hundred and twenty seconds. And let me tell you friends it went like – that.

I went out there with my team and swam my absolute heart out. I gave it everything in me for my teammates, for myself and for my country. I pushed my mind to a limit beyond what my body thought was possible. Every ounce of effort, love, hard work, passion, and persistence went into that swim. And it was over, both swims were over quicker than I ever could have imagined.

As I finished and looked up to my family cheer squad, jumping with elation in the stands, I was beaming with pride. Pride that they got to have this moment. Pride that they got to experience this beauty. Because, for them, it was about this. Being there for me. Claiming and proclaiming that their daughter, little sister, friend, girl-friend had just competed at the Olympics.

But, as I pulled my fatigued body out of the water and walked my lactic-filled legs up on stage, I was reminded of my epiphany before I headed into Olympic Team Trials.

It was never about the Olympics.

Now you may think I am crazy? "You got us this far in the book, your calling yourself the Unlikely Olympian and telling me it isn't even about that?"

Yes I am.

Because what I was reminded of, standing there up on stage, having felt like the memory of my Olympic swim was already slipping through the fingers of my mind is that **I had already done it.**

Nowadays, as a society, we get so darn focused on the END GOAL. The thing we are working towards, that thing that we are trying to achieve. But when we are all so laser focused on the end goal we are ALL MISSING THE POINT!

People say go after your dreams, you can do anything, do the impossible, but we all get so tied up in thinking about that impossible, that dream, that goal that we don't realize most important part.

> You achieve your dream in the
> process of going after it.
> Truly going after it. When you give it your
> everything & have nothing to hold back.
> Because it is about who you BECOME
> on the journey, not about what you achieve,
> at the end of the day.

Sitting there that evening a few days before Olympic team trials, staring the possibility of "failure" in the face, it hit me that it was never about the Olympics.

It was about PROVING to myself that "I am ENOUGH, I am CAPABLE, I am WORTHY".

It is about every little experience that added up along the way, that brought me to where I am today. It is about every moment. Every experience, every memory. Every person you met and every lesson you learned.

Because life is not like the Olympic Games, life is like the journey to get there.

We don't work our whole lives to have a resume, a checklist of things that we have accomplished to take with you to the grave. BUT THAT IS WHAT SO MANY OF US DO!

We put our head down and work our butts off until we get to this THING that we are aiming for. Because, when we get there, we will be accomplished. When we get there, we will be worthy. When we get there, we will show ourselves that we are enough.

NO, my beautiful friends.

You see, that is the BEAUTY about what I learned. What I experienced. I achieved my dream through the process of going after it. The Olympics was just the cherry on top.

You may be thinking – well that is easy for YOU to say because you actually did do it! You actually went to the Olympics; you are an Olympian.

That is true but that didn't matter. Because if I didn't do it I would still be the person I am today, just without the title of an Olympian. The experience, the learning, the person I became on the PROCESS, on the JOURNEY to the Games is the person I am today. If you were to have taken everything else away and only given me the seven-minute experience competing at the Games – I would not be the same, loving, determined, caring, fulfilled DK that has smashed through her limiting self-beliefs and wades in an abundance of gratitude and love for life.

> I am who I am NOT because of what I achieve but because of what I experienced in the process of becoming my true self

You see amigas, you can-NOT Fail. When you do it right, when you follow the steps, through clarity you will ONLY have success. Because success is in the ever-present. Success isn't at the end.

1. Be **Clear** on your Limiting Self-Beliefs.

2. **Love** what you do & do what you **LOVE.**

3. Realize that **Adversity** is part of the process to make you grow.

4. The universe **Requires** you to ACT on what you believe is possible.

5. Constantly work on **Improving** along the way through self-awareness.

6. Have **Thankfulness** throughout the journey with gratitude and presence.

7. **YOU** will realize that you are already living the dream.

It is not rocket science. It is just a shift in perspective. The method I have described here is nothing that you can't do. You have ALL this inside you if you choose to believe. When you open your eyes to see the world through different glasses you can do it too.

I was a girl who thought nothing of herself, who struggled with self-belief and bathed in self-hatred. I wasn't super-gifted or talented, but I was passionate. And I listened to the whisper inside my soul that believed that there was more for me in this world than my limiting self-beliefs made me think.

I am not special. I just an ordinary girl who tapped into what is inside all of us, to create a possibility for myself. And I truly believe, with every ounce of my heart, that I didn't do it for me. I did it for you. Because, like I said, I am your best friend, motivator and biggest cheerleader because I know YOU can do it too.

You are destined to.

Now go out there and be your own Unlikely Olympian.